Dressing the Home

The Private Spaces of Top Fashion Designers

Dressing the Home

The Private Spaces of Top Fashion Designers

■ By Marie Bariller
Photographs by Guillaume de Laubier
Foreword by Domenico Dolce & Stefano Gabbana

Abrams, New York

Contents

■ List of Fashion Designers

Foreword

"There's no place like home!" says Dorothy in *The Wizard of Oz,* when she finds herself amid everything she holds dearest: her house, her family, and her dreams come true.

■ Indeed, if we think of the story of our home, we cannot help telling a love story, never banal or dull, filled with passion and character, with choices and small gestures, with daily actions and sensations that stay with us forever.

■ Creativity, whether in fashion or interior design, uses the language of passion, which comes from the heart. To create a style or a setting for living always takes us back into ourselves.

■ It is not always easy to explain this strong, tight, even unbreakable bond that exists between creativity and the art of living. It is a very Italian bond, certainly, but also doubtless a universal one, common to all those who approach life with enthusiasm and in a spirit of innovation.

■ Lifestyle is a mixture of imagination, skill, and also chance, and always with this quest for beauty and truth. And it is the same striving for beauty, serenity, and wonder that lies at the root of each of our creative choices—from cutting the cloth for an evening dress to hanging a painting by Andy Warhol next to a votive statue of the Virgin.

■ For each of our choices says something about us and reveals a part of our hearts. When we saw the Roquebrune house for the first time, for example, we were immediately fascinated by the extraordinary setting of the garden, which looks out over the sea, and by the geometric, rational spaces of the rooms, which seem to offer the viewer a theatrical range of possibilities. Apart from the beauty of the place, there was also a kind of energy, which eventually persuaded us to buy this house: the dynamism and enthusiasm that are part of the Côte d'Azur, with its myths made up of diamonds and yachts, secret passion and royal luxury, the luminosity of the Mediterranean and the ostentation of Monte Carlo.

■ And for us, having always loved the *dolce vita,* this waking dream turned out to be the chief stimulus that made us transform this house in the Dolce & Gabbana style, to render personal and welcoming a place that was already perfect in itself. Perfect, but empty—where were life, creativity, sensations? Now, this was a place that was simultaneously simple and special. Like all houses. Like all dreams.

■ Simple and special: It was around these two poles that our style developed, beginning with a luxury that combined romanticism with irony, always executed with care and professionalism. A worthy heir to the traditions, inspirations, and dreams that breathe energy and happiness into people.

■ It is precisely thanks to this union of contrasting elements that this true, dynamic, innovative, personal, and creative style was born: the eyes of the North and the heart of the South, the baroque and Purism, popular art and Art Nouveau, Neorealism and Pop Art, black and white, dream and reality.

■ Sometimes a little imagination and boldness, creativity and tenacity, are enough to make even waking dreams come true.

■ As you will discover in this book.

Domenico Dolce and Stefano Gabbana

Preface

■ During the first decade of the twentieth century, the couturier Paul Poiret changed the structure of the clothing industry and brought a new dimension to his profession, giving it its present role and place in society. A highly cultured man, drawing on his view of the world and its development, Poiret's researches led him beyond simply working on clothes. A visionary, Paul Poiret was the first couturier to take his creations into the world of decoration, even going so far as to open a school of decorative art.

■ At the dawn of the twenty-first century, generations of fashion designers have emulated their illustrious predecessor in their quest for a certain art of living. Interior decoration is indeed a natural vector of the illustration of a style, and allows an aesthetic vision to be communicated via a place, rather than simply a garment.

■ Because of this, I felt a natural desire to illustrate these parallels between the world of fashion and that of interior decoration. In this book, some of the most talented fashion designers, living in cities from Rome to Delhi and from New York to Paris, reveal to us their points of view, their similarities, and their differences. Those for whom the details of a garment's cut, the nuances of a color, the magic of a color combination, or the texture and the appearance of a fabric are integral elements of their creations can also express themselves in the same way through interior decoration. Their roots, their sources of inspiration, and their cultures add diversity and creative richness to the places where they live.

■ The choice of décor is never neutral, and reveals individuality that is the result of time, experience, goals in life, culture, affinities, and means. To visit the homes of these fashion designers—as varied as they are singular—is to see revealed a neoclassical ambiance, an eighteenth-century atmosphere, an explosion of colors, a profusion of objects, or pure modernity, each bearing the unmistakable and unique stamps of these artists, who leave their marks on everything with which they surround themselves.

■ These aesthetes with inexhaustible imaginations, often the initiators of trends, manage to surprise us once again and to make us dream, as they dress places just as they dress bodies. Their fluency in both of these ways of expressing beauty is clearly conveyed in this book.

Marie Bariller

Manish
Arora

Filled with an infectious, colorful enthusiasm, the dazzling collections of Manish Arora humorously reveal his vision of a flamboyant, modern India. In his house in Delhi, he shows the art of living in a riot of color and patterns, where gaiety finds its inspiration in the flourishing culture of the Orient.

If you were a color, what would you be?
Fluorescent pink.

Where did you acquire your taste for interior decoration?

There are obviously similarities, and a certain interaction between my taste in interior decoration and in fashion. I like to be surrounded by colors, both in my garments and at home; they make me happy and energetic.

Are your sources of inspiration the same both for fashion and interior decoration?

Different ideas guide me when I design fashion collections, but India remains my chief source of inspiration, now and always. It is essentially there that I make my designs.

Are you interested in architecture? Who is your favorite architect?

I am interested in design and, in a more general sense, in all beautiful things that awaken the senses, especially painting, music, and architecture. I especially like the dazzling, original architecture of Antoni Gaudí.

What is your favorite decorative style?

I like Art Deco a lot.

If you were a house, which would you be?

Mine.

If you were an era?

The twenty-first century.

If you were an item of furniture, what would you be?

A sofa.

If you were a room, which would you be?

My dining room.

What are your favorite color combinations in interior design? Are they the same as those you use in fashion?
Red, blue, fuchsia, and black are my basic colors, but in my fashion collections my palette is infinite.

What are your favorite materials?
The use of plastic can be very interesting in interior decoration.

Do fabrics play an important part in your interior decoration? How do you use them?
Fabrics are so important to me in interior decoration that I have even covered my walls in them . . . and it's wonderful. I also like to use some prints that I have designed for my various collections. Without fabrics, the very concept of interior decoration would be incomplete as far as I'm concerned.

In fashion, a cut of the scissors or a seam is of crucial importance. What aspects are most important in interior decoration?
Various objets d'art, objects from collections, and souvenirs brought back from many journeys visibly complement the interior décor of a place.

As a fashion designer, what you create differs according to the season. Does this encourage you to change the décor of your house often?
I would like to be able to change the décor according to my many desires and inspirations, but this would mean living in total confusion. On the other hand, certain pieces of décor, directly inspired by my past fashion designs or by certain times in my life, find their place in my rooms.

What sort of atmosphere do you like to create in a house?
I like the ambiance of utter comfort in which I can relax and recover every day.

Which is your favorite room at home?
I love my dining room on the terrace.

What small everyday pleasures does your home give you?
My favorite moments are those I spend alone in the morning, doing yoga, and those spent having a drink with my friends in the evening.

Do you have a motto in interior decoration?
No, not really.

Is decorating a house the same as clothing a body?
The garment must adapt to the body in motion, just like a place or a piece of furniture must serve the function it is given. Moreover, in both cases it is a matter of deciding just to what degree function actually matters. ∎

If you were a piece of music, what would you be?
Lounge music.

A painting?
Leonardo da Vinci's Last Supper.

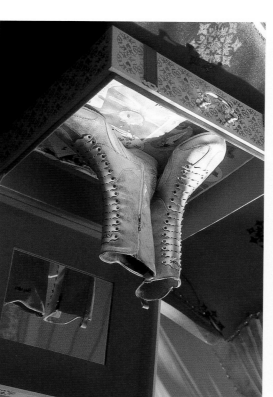

A fabric?
Lycra.

Damiano
Biella

Tucked away in the heart of Rome, the baroque apartment of Damiano Biella,

artistic director of the celebrated Escada fashion house, pays fervent homage to a fusion of

styles from different eras. Past and present echo each other in a subtle balance whose studied

aestheticism illustrates the Italian designer's refinement and love of art.

If you were a color, what would you be?
Chocolate.

If you were an item of furniture?
A chaise longue.

If you were a house, what would you be?
An English manor house.

Where did you acquire your taste for interior decoration?

I love fashion above everything else; it has always been my passion. Interior decoration is a style exercise very like a game for me, for it isn't really my work. However, decorating a bedroom is like creating a collection: Colors need to be combined, and elements and materials blended together . . . and I adore making sketches for house interiors.

Are your sources of inspiration the same both for fashion and interior decoration?

Not necessarily, but it is true that I often find them in the same places: on a journey in a city, in the mountains, or by the sea. The same elements, removed from their original settings, can sometimes be used for collections or for interior decoration. Fashion itself can be a source of inspiration for interior decoration.

Are you interested in architecture? Who is your favorite architect?

Certainly: I like the architect Tadao Ando very much. He works with great respect for the environment and very elegantly. I greatly appreciate his contemporary spirit and the clarity of his lines. I am also very fond of Italian Renaissance architecture, and particularly that of Andrea Palladio.

What is your favorite decorative style?

I am attracted to eclecticism. I adore the fusion of different periods, the old and the contemporary: hanging seventeenth-century court portraits (a veritable passion of mine) on the walls, and combining 1960s and 1970s furniture with modern design items.

What are your favorite color combinations in interior design? Are they the same as those you use in fashion?

Colors account for a very large part of my work. In my home, apart from the dining room (which I had fun painting in red lacquer), I prefer to live among the most neutral tones—different beiges, ivory, black, and white, which have always been fundamental in my life, but also chocolate brown, which is, I think, my favorite color. Paintings, books, and flowers bring their own touches of color.

What are your favorite materials?

I don't have favorite materials. The blend of materials is what interests me more: for example, baroque carved wood with steel.

Do fabrics play an important part in your interior decoration? How do you use them?

Like colors, fabrics have a less important role in my interior decoration than they have in my work. They are more like touches, rather than major pieces that you notice as soon as you enter. I like the severity of velvet in dark colors such as black, chocolate brown, and dark blue, or, by contrast, very pale beige velvet. Also, I love black-and-white graphic stripes.

In fashion, a cut of the scissors or a seam is of crucial importance. What aspects are most important in interior decoration?

Symmetry is the most important detail in my apartment, and the very foundation of my personality. I associate symmetry with a certain equilibrium in decoration. For me to feel at ease in a place—even a hotel room—I prefer there to be two identical objects, such as two sofas, or two tables.

As a fashion designer, what you create differs according to the season. Does this encourage you to change the décor of your house often?

It is indeed often by moving around the furniture in a room that one changes one's perception of that space. Very regularly—about once a month—I move a sofa, or two chairs, or perhaps a painting. I also like to change the color of an area of wall, or fabrics, to place, or not, cushions on the sofa, arrange a new bunch of flowers, or bring in a candle with a new fragrance. These are not radical changes, but they are enough to make me feel better.

If you were an era, which would you be?
Tomorrow.

If you were a piece of music?
Something by Marin Marais.

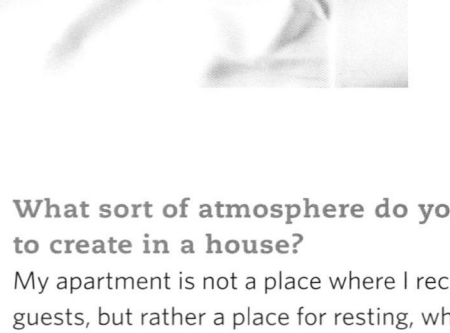

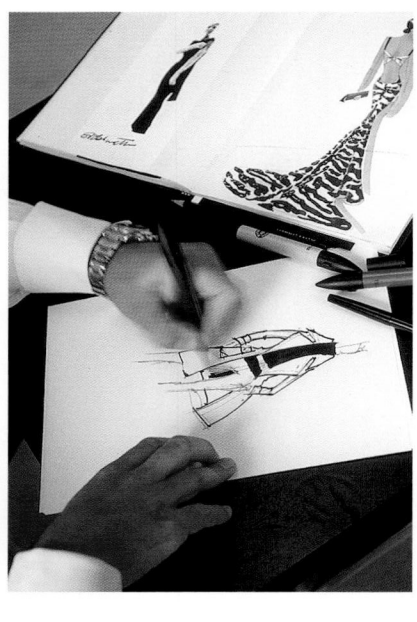

What sort of atmosphere do you like to create in a house?

My apartment is not a place where I receive guests, but rather a place for resting, where I go to live with my small family and my friends. This place must above all be warm; the colors and the light are never violent.

Which is your favorite room at home?

That depends on the day. In fact, I like all the rooms in my apartment.

What small everyday pleasures does your home give you?

I love eating breakfast on the sofa; the view over the rooftops of Rome and the wonderful light enchant me every day. I like hearing all the noises of the city: the craftsmen, the little Vespas . . . in short, the heart of Rome.

Do you have a motto in interior decoration?

Make yourself comfortable. It applies to me as much as to the friends who come here. Above all, people should not be afraid to sit down in case they break something.

Is decorating a house the same as clothing a body?

It is exactly the same. In fashion design, you need an overall vision. When you imagine a shirt, you think of what goes with it, how it will be shown, the places where it will be sold, who will wear it, and how it will be arranged with other garments bought elsewhere. . . . It is exactly the same with interior decoration: a combination of elements, materials, colors, fragrances, and light. The senses are alive in both these spheres. ■

If you were a painting, what would you be?
A Flemish portrait.

Vanessa Bruno

In her Parisian apartment, Vanessa Bruno diffuses the same natural delicacy that has been the hallmark of her style from the beginning. Like her collections, the softness of her handmade fabrics and the harmonies of pastel tints—here combined with the pale-colored wood of Scandinavian furniture—perfectly illustrate the modern, unaffected femininity of her designs.

If you were a painting, what would you be?
A watercolor.

If you were a house, what would you be?

■ A big Gustavian-style house by the sea or by a lake.

32

Where did you acquire your taste for interior decoration?

I think I have always liked that. . . . I get this passion certainly from my mother, who could not stop herself picking up things more or less wherever she went. We always had to find a second-hand shop, or get up early to go to the market. I have this taste for objects, but above all the desire to appropriate them, to combine them so that they do not become museum pieces. . . . They must fit into the space.

Are your sources of inspiration the same both for fashion and interior decoration?

It is true that I am very fond of handmade craftsmanship, both in fashion and in decoration. Textiles are important to me. Whether we are talking about a curtain or a piece of fabric, my attention focuses first on what will demand extremely skillful work. I like natural wood and Scandinavian design; it has left its mark on me. I also like combining different periods, as in my work, when I put together a collection . . . but at the same time the guiding principle is delicate things, made by hand.

Are you interested in architecture? Who is your favorite architect?

I like architecture very much. I think Jean Nouvel is a very great architect. I am also very fond of the architects of the 1960s. They had a way of harmonizing space and the setting with straight-sided shapes, great glazed bays, which could at the same time seem austere. . . . But all these houses around Los Angeles are nevertheless rather superb. I love it when architecture makes way for the art of living.

I am also very attracted by the oldest architecture. . . . When I walk in the streets of London, I like all these little Victorian houses with their moldings and cozy quality very much.

What is your favorite decorative style?

I have great difficulty liking uniformity of style in an interior, where everything is perfect. Unexpected combinations are more alive. However, I have a weakness for the Scandinavian style: Gustavian or 1960s design, Jacobsen or Werner Panton. They combine well.

If you were an item of furniture, what would you be?

A comfortable bed with lots of cushions.

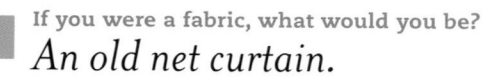
If you were a fabric, what would you be?
An old net curtain.

What are your favorite color combinations in interior design? Are they the same as those you use in fashion?

I like to play with nuances by mixing a very light color with another. For example, in the room with the floor tiles, I dyed a natural, unbleached material with sienna to give the walls an aged feeling in harmony with the tiles. It's very subtle, but it gives the wall a feeling of depth. Whether in my fashion designs or in interior decoration, I like grayish, faded, dirty pastel colors.

What are your favorite materials?

I like different kinds of wood: solid wood, rough wood. I like painting very simple furniture in a matte finish to make it blend in with the walls of a room.

By contrast, I also quite like lacquered objects or pieces of furniture that shine, as well as tiles.

Do fabrics play an important part in your interior decoration? How do you use them?

It is important to me to choose the fabric of a sofa, cushion, or rug—which I like to move around regularly. I love it when there is harmony between oneself and a fabric. A cushion that brings a certain softness, for example, or the texture of the sheets when one gets into bed. I also like using doilies as curtains, as in my living room. They are so intricate, so delicate. And the light that passes through them further emphasizes this delicacy. This creates a peaceful atmosphere; it's pleasant.

In fashion, a cut of the scissors or a seam is of crucial importance. What aspects are most important in interior decoration?

Volume and texture interest me. I love digging out little-known furniture by Scandinavian designers. I pay great attention to volume and details, such as the shape of the feet or particular finishes.

I like to make things my own, as long as this does not go to absurd lengths. To buy IKEA kitchen furniture and repaint it to one's taste, that's making things one's own. It's like when I look at a woman wearing garments that I think I recognize: She wears them in her own way and her bearing then becomes highly personal.

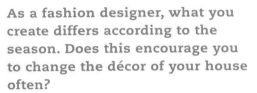

As a fashion designer, what you create differs according to the season. Does this encourage you to change the décor of your house often?

I never say to myself "I'm going to change the décor." I am very faithful to my clothes, objects, and certain pieces of furniture that I have owned for a very long time. On the other hand, I may move objects or furniture about; I modify things little by little. But I have the willpower not to overload the décor.

What sort of atmosphere do you like to create in a house?

I believe in conviviality. I like people to feel welcome, at their ease, immediately. Sometimes one goes into apartments where one does not dare touch anything, not even to sit down. I like the sensation of a place where there is some life. . . . With the children, my wooden dining room table has received many knocks, but it doesn't matter . . . it's alive.

Which is your favorite room at home?

The living room, I think. I entertain my friends a lot, and I like this large room where everyone is gathered together, with music.

What small everyday pleasures does your home give you?

There are two things I particularly like. First, flowers; for me, they are like a beautiful painting. I like to arrange a bouquet and find a place for it, or put a flower in the bedroom. . . . A room then acquires another dimension. I also have another ritual. When I get home, especially in winter when it is already dark, I light the candles. That's when I really say to myself: "There we are. I'm home." It's funny, because my daughter has now started to perform this ritual, which I got from my mother.

Do you have a motto in interior decoration?

No, I don't. . . . Maybe just to feel good at home.

Is decorating a house the same as clothing a body?

I'd rather draw a parallel with music. Music, whether at work or at home, helps me to disconnect from everyday reality. ■

If you were a color, what would you be?
White.

If you were a piece of music?
The album Tapestry *by Carole King.*

Patrick Cox

Famous London shoe designer Patrick Cox has a sense of humor that never deserts him when he creates his unfailingly original shoe collections. In his London house, his feeling for detail has naturally led him to surround himself with objects he has collected over the years. From the Greco-Roman style to the Empire style and that of the 1960s, different periods mingle in an atmosphere of unrestrained refinement.

If you were an era, which would you be?
Ancient Rome.

If you were a house, what would you be?

An early nineteenth–century house, with fine proportions, high ceilings, and handsome details.

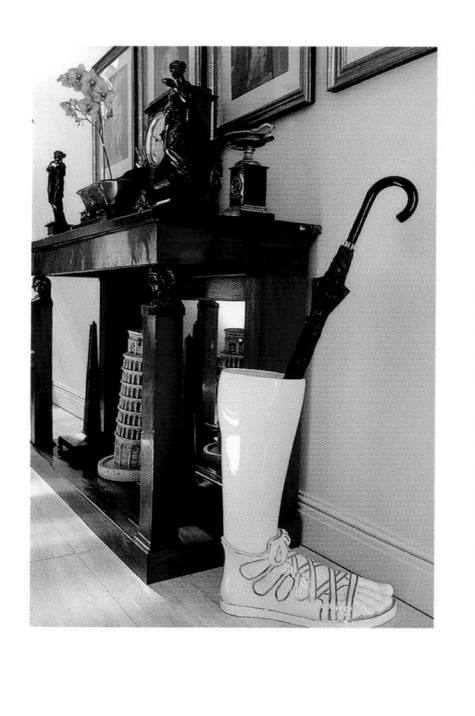

Where did you acquire your taste for interior decoration?

I probably got my taste in interior decoration from my travels. I am like a sponge: I adore reading, watching films, and visiting museums and exhibitions. I am always in search of new things in many spheres.

Are your sources of inspiration the same both for fashion and interior decoration?

In fashion, my inspiration comes from pop culture—the 1960s and the following years— whereas in interior design, my influences are much broader. I like the atmosphere of the twentieth century and the present as much as the Neoclassical period or the Empire. My inspiration for interior design is more historical than traditional.

Are you interested in architecture? Who is your favorite architect?

I don't really have a favorite architect; however, I appreciate a certain kind of imposing, masculine architecture, and I would say that the Greco-Roman style, classicism under Louis XIV, and the architecture of [Andrea] Palladio are styles that inspire me a great deal. . . . Palladio might be my favorite, because everything leads me back to him.

What is your favorite decorative style?

I quite like very pure contemporary lines, but to live in a minimalist place would bore me deeply. I prefer to combine the antiques that I have been collecting for many years with the modern. I think a house should reflect the interests and personality of the occupant, but it takes time to gather together the objects one likes around oneself. I find that many houses seem to be representations, for people tend to buy ready-made "looks" that, at bottom, don't work.

What are your favorite color combinations in interior design? Are they the same as those you use in fashion?

When designing my collection, I work chiefly in black, heightened with bright colors, whereas at home I prefer warmer, more neutral shades.

What are your favorite materials?

I love playing with the contrast of gilded wood against travertine, or combining brilliant chrome with dark brown marble.

If you were an item of furniture?
An Empire chandelier.

If you were a room, what would you be?
The dining room.

If you were a color?
Taupe.

Do fabrics play an important part in your interior decoration? How do you use them?
I like very luxurious fabrics—velvets, hide, and leather.

In fashion, a cut of the scissors or a seam is of crucial importance. What aspects are most important in interior decoration?
Quality and patience are essential. If you do not possess them, your house will look like a showroom devoid of personality. It took me many years to gather together the pieces I care about. In my first apartment, I had bought a magnificent French chandelier before I bought my bed—simply because I had found it first! One should not hurry to find things: They arrive when they are meant to arrive.

As a fashion designer, what you create differs according to the season. Does this encourage you to change the décor of your house often?
The central point when decorating one's house is that there must be a sense of constancy. In my case, this comes from all these pieces from antique collections, bought one by one. I would not like it if my house appeared transitory, and yet at the same time, it is also in constant movement.

What sort of atmosphere do you like to create in a house?
Comfort is so important. For example, the ground-floor living room is where I like to sit and read peacefully for hours. I like airy, light places, and I like ordered places.

Which is your favorite room at home?
I would say certainly the living room; it is the room where I spend the most time. It is a space where one can enjoy eating, drinking, and talking, or watching a film. It is a very versatile room.

What small everyday pleasures does your home give you?

Sleeping! The fact that I travel so much makes me really appreciate sleeping in my own bed.

Do you have a motto in interior decoration?

Order and symmetry, to follow in the footsteps of Palladian or Greco-Roman architecture. Wherever you are in the house, you will always see a north–south or east–west axis in the interior decoration. I like the logic that brings to a place; I am rather obsessed by that.

Is decorating a house the same as clothing a body?

Everything must be of the best quality, fit perfectly, and attain its goal of providing comfort. ∎

If you were a piece of music, what would you be?

Disco music by Studio 54.

If you were a fabric?

I would not be a fabric, but python skin.

If you were a painting, what would you be?
Electric Chair *by Andy Warhol.*

Dolce
& Gabbana

Black and white, white and black haughtily dominate the house of the flamboyant Domenico Dolce and Stefano Gabbana in the south of France. Mink and muslin on lava stone, a marriage of styles and graphic interplay orchestrated by zebra-striped hides call to mind the dazzling, highly contrasting collections of these two Italian designers. This is where the Mediterranean attains magnificence.

If you were a fabric, what would you be?

S.G.: *Slightly torn denim.*
D.D.: *Black velvet.*

If you were a color, what would you be?

S.G.: *Black; we do not see it as the absence of color, but as the sum of all colors and hues that exist in nature.*

D.D.: *Unquestionably black or white— absolute, strong, intense colors.*

Where did you acquire your taste for interior decoration?

STEFANO GABBANA: There is undoubtedly a very close link between our fashion designs and the décor of our houses. Each Dolce & Gabbana space, whether it be public (like showrooms and shops) or private, contains a whole series of elements that speak clearly about us and our style. And at the same time, each space is different and unique, because we respect its basic circumstances and allow ourselves to fall under the spell of its history.

DOMENICO DOLCE: Each of our collections has been thought through like a film. There is a story, a dream, characters, and an ending. And each collection is different from the previous one, even if it comprises all the elements of the Dolce & Gabbana style. Exactly the same is true of the houses: Portofino, Stromboli, Milan, and Roquebrune are unquestionably structured and conceived to reflect our world, but our inspiration has, in each case, come together with and blended with genius loci, to create surprising and totally unique situations. It is like a work of art, a special garment, or like the famous "master stroke" of genius that transforms a collection into a success.

If you were a house, what would you be?

S.G.: *Mine! I don't care which!*

D.D.: *This house in Roquebrune represents me perfectly.*

Are your sources of inspiration the same both for fashion and interior decoration?

S. G.: They are the same, but only up to a point. As far as fashion is concerned, our prime source of inspiration is always the street: Thanks to direct, careful observation of everything that goes on around us, we always have an exact idea of what people expect, of the way they want to dress. Later, we complement this "informal" source of inspiration with ideas that come to us from the world of cinema: Hollywood stars, with their innate glamour, but also Italian neorealist cinema, with the power of its contrasts and landscapes, and with these courageous Mediterranean women whom directors such as [Roberto] Rossellini and [Luchino] Visconti portrayed so well.

D. D.: In interior decoration, on the other hand, sources of inspiration are a little different. There are still evocations of Sicily and of the baroque, and hints of the Mediterranean. But we add—both Stefano and I—various touches, which sometimes differ widely from each other. For example, we alternate designer furniture made exclusively for us with chairs or tables picked up in second-hand shops; we place the work of great designers alongside the simplest of creations; and we play with colors and irony without ever losing sight of the soul, the spirit of each house. Whereas in fashion we shape the garments, houses, by contrast, "suggest" to us how we might proceed with interior design.

Are you interested in architecture? Who is your favorite architect?

D. D.: I have always been fascinated by architecture. I especially like Ettore Sottsass; indeed, we have been inspired by his conception of architecture to create certain accessories. I also like the poetic rationalism of Le Corbusier and the simplicity of David Chipperfield, as well as the surprising taste of Ferruccio Laviani.

S. G.: I think architecture is an art form, like fashion. At the moment, I am very interested in Ron Arad: I am fascinated by his constant experimentation with materials. And naturally, I find that there are some great architects in the past, such as Bernini or Piermarini, who were true geniuses.

What is your favorite decorative style?

D. D.: I don't have a favorite style. In the way I conceive interior decoration, I see an eclecticism of styles rather than a single, standardized one. I very much like the psychedelic illustrations of the 1960s and 1970s, combined, though, with elegant lines and three-dimensional shapes, and with fabrics decorated with animal designs or velvet. And all of this filtered through a rigorous rationalism without, however, overdoing it.

S. G.: I am heavily influenced by baroque taste. I like contrasts, both in style and in materials: for example, extremely pure, sober polished steel combined with pink marble decorated with arabesques, with gold, and black opaline—and all of this interpreted in an ironic way. I love posters and graphic decorations.

What are your favorite color combinations in interior design? Are they the same as those you use in fashion?

D. D.: I find that black is, absolutely, the most elegant color. An ebony chest of drawers is, in my view, highly stylish, just as a black evening dress can be.

S. G.: Art and architecture have always been a great source of inspiration for me. Similarly, the fashion that we create influences the way I see other art forms. Animal motifs, black, and gold are the colors I prefer, both for clothes and for furniture.

What are your favorite materials?

D. D.: Basaltina, natural stone, and black opaline, as well as gold mosaics and reflecting surfaces.

S. G.: I like gold, too, but also marble and steel. In all my houses there is always wooden furniture, whether valuable items or those picked up in second-hand shops.

Do fabrics play an important part in your interior decoration? How do you use them?

D. D.: Fabrics are fundamental in interior decoration. I choose them with the same care and attention I bring to choosing fabrics for our designs.

S. G.: Coverings and hangings must be precious and elegant to make a house glamorous. Velvet, astrakhan hides, and animal motifs beautify, furnish, and decorate in a sublime way.

In fashion, a cut of the scissors or a seam is of crucial importance. What aspects are most important in interior decoration?

D. D.: Attention to details is equally important in interior decoration. I think one should take particular care with proportions, and with the blend of styles and materials so as to produce a harmonious effect, which is both striking and reassuring.

S. G.: Making the most of light and contrasts, as we have done at Roquebrune. It is through contrasts that one achieves harmony. Our houses are "cultivated" with care and passion, to convey something honestly and affectionately about us, in the same way as our garments are studied, I would even say loved, in the tiniest details.

As fashion designers, what you create differs according to the season. Does this encourage you to change the décor of your houses often?

D. D.: What inspires us changes from season to season, thus influencing our designs. It is completely normal that, from time to time, I also feel like changing the décor of my house, even if it isn't exactly every season!

S. G.: Of course, even though my personal style and my taste remain unchanged over time.

What sort of atmosphere do you like to create in a house?

D. D.: A warm, welcoming atmosphere in which I can receive my family and my friends, but also something festive and original. A protective, fascinating, and slightly surprising environment.

S. G.: I like to think that my house is a tribute to beauty and elegance, and that it represents the way I am. Showiness and simplicity.

If you were an era, which would you be?

s.g.: *The present. Or, rather, the present, but looking more to the future.*

d.d.: *I feel the same. We are accustomed to experiencing the present with an eye firmly fixed on the future, and I find this is the best way to continue giving ourselves, and others, what we do best: a dream.*

Which is your favorite room at home?

D. D.: The dining room, a place for meeting and sharing meals with family and friends.

S. G.: The living room, because it is the room where I spend the most time relaxing, alone or with friends. And naturally the bedroom, where I can take refuge after a hectic day!

What small everyday pleasures does your home give you?

D. D.: To get up in the morning and walk with my dogs in a flower-filled garden, with a breathtaking view over the sea.

S. G.: Switching off my mobile phone and relaxing on the sofa watching television or reading a magazine, raising my eyes from time to time to see an extraordinary view, between the sky and the sea.

Do you have a motto in interior decoration?

S. G.: I try to surround myself with a kind of beauty that brings pleasure and cheers, without which I would feel as if I was living in a museum.

D. D.: Ensure that your house says something about you, but above all that it says something to you.

Is decorating a house the same as clothing a body?

S. G.: Yes and no. A house, like a body, needs precise, made-to-measure details, and demands shapes that heighten the strong points while softening the weak ones. A special, personal interior décor can make a house splendid, in the same way that a beautiful dress can make someone's body marvelous or desirable. And even houses "live," almost as if they were human beings.

But I think that the parallels end there: A human body changes shape and proportions, and is more subject to changes in taste and fashion. A house has a rigid structure which is difficult to change, which offers opportunities but also imposes limitations. ∎

If you were a painting, what would you be?

S.G.: *A Passion or an Ecstasy from the Mannerist period, or perhaps a painting by Andy Warhol.*
D.D.: *Something by Julian Schnabel.*

Jacopo
Etro

Soft swirls of cashmere and refined, colorful striped fabrics have made sumptuous contributions to the renown of the Italian fashion house Etro, and Jacopo Etro has traveled the world in search of them. His collections of unusual objects, his handsome books, which cover the walls, and the warm shades of his Milan apartment embody his enthusiasm for travels to far-off lands.

If you were an era, which would you be?
The French sixteenth century.

If you were a painting, what would you be?

A Vanitas.

A house?

A country house.

Where did you acquire your taste for interior decoration?
My taste in interior design is very varied. Recently, I traveled to Uzbekistan, above Iran; it is a place that benefits from a very vigorous textile and historical tradition, and where people still dress according to old traditions. The country is on the Silk Road, which formerly linked China with Europe, and along which merchants transported the most prestigious fabrics.

Are your sources of inspiration the same both for fashion and interior decoration?
Imagination is fundamental: Without it, it is impossible to combine fabrics, cuts, and colors. The fact that I am constantly searching for something stimulating, in my travels, in my reading, and in the world around me, means I am constantly in motion and conveying my feelings to people.

Are you interested in architecture? Who is your favorite architect?
Yes. Frank Gehry is very eclectic.

What is your favorite decorative style?
I don't like minimalism. In my house, I like to have color and richness; I need to feel warm, pampered, protected.

What are your favorite color combinations in interior design? Are they the same as those you use in fashion?
I like warm colors that convey emotion, combined with slightly modern geometric elements. My style has always been the same throughout my life.

What are your favorite materials?
Natural materials, because they last forever.

Do fabrics play an important part in your interior decoration? How do you use them?
I have a great passion for fabrics, and the constant quest I mentioned earlier is the basis from which I offer interesting, attractive fabrics that have come from different cultures. It is a fascinating journey, because it can take me to India, to the Orient, in contact with very ancient civilizations and peoples rich in tradition.

In fashion, a cut of the scissors or a seam is of crucial importance. What aspects are most important in interior decoration?
I place most importance on harmony between colors and patterns.

If you were a fabric, what would you be?
Velvet.

If you were a color, what would you be?
Red.

As a fashion designer, what you create differs according to the season. Does this encourage you to change the décor of your house often?

I tend instead to add new pieces of furniture and remove others.

What sort of atmosphere do you like to create in a house?

A warm ambiance, always. I like to invite different kinds of people to dinner—a maximum of ten at any one time—to talk informally, maybe sitting on big cushions. It is essential to offer one's guests moments of intimacy and happiness. Perfumes are very important for creating a perfect, relaxed atmosphere. I prefer ambergris or incense and squat, noninvasive candles to promote conversation between guests; no scents that are too strong or flowery perfumes.

Which is your favorite room at home?

My living room, which contains the library where I keep all my art books.

What small everyday pleasures does your home give you?

Relaxing in my bathroom while listening to classical music.

Do you have a motto in interior decoration?

Less is not necessarily more.

Is decorating a house the same as clothing a body?

No, if anything, I am clothing someone's soul. ∎

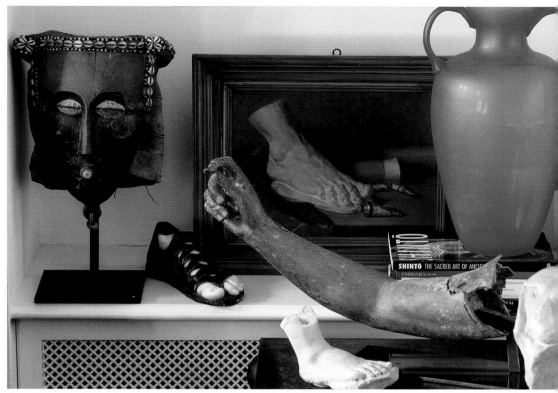

If you were an item of furniture, what would you be?

A handsome light.

A room?

A library.

Loulou de la Falaise

The muse of Yves Saint Laurent and creator of an impressive, bewitching jewelry line with floral, pictorial, and ethnic motifs under her own name, Loulou de la Falaise has set up an artist's studio that reflects her personality. Perched under the rooftops of Paris, this place—which is simultaneously grandiose and unconventional—combines elegance and imagination in a natural way.

If you were a color, what would you be?
Red.

Where did you acquire your taste for interior decoration?

This taste really developed rather gradually, over several house moves and from ideas about certain décors. When I entered my apartment for the first time, I felt good in this artist's studio. I have always lived, ever since childhood—with my parents, we lived in a New York loft—in atypical, unconventional places. I don't like partitions, for example. As far as decoration is concerned, I had at first imagined a Saharan atmosphere in beige shades, then blue and white for a maritime ambiance.

Are your sources of inspiration the same both for fashion and interior decoration?

I'm fairly consistent in my tastes on the whole. I like bright, multihued fabrics and colors. Anything can inspire me, whether it's a journey or a crack in a wall. Sometimes I can even transform an undesirable object into a desirable one. To find inspiration in everything can become automatic if you allow this little machine in your head to work.

If you were a fabric, what would you be?

A prayer mat.

Are you interested in architecture? Who is your favorite architect?

I like architecture, and great architects of all periods impress me. The building where I live is one of the pieces of architecture that I like very much. The interior architecture of each apartment is more or less identical, but there is always something different.

Building sites attract me immensely . . . the feeling of progression, when the building rises from the ground. And then there are the great urban planners who employ different architects to avoid monotony. No uniformity: That's my principle in life.

What is your favorite decorative style?

I am very attracted to the 1930s . . . but above all I like blends of styles . . . things that have nothing to do with each other.

What are your favorite color combinations in interior design? Are they the same as those you use in fashion?

I have a strong attraction to combinations of reds, orange . . . all shades of red. It is a color that recurs constantly in my designs and in my apartment. My shop is adorned with red furniture, a red carpet; it isn't really a voluntary thing but an irresistible attraction. . . . It turns out that when I like an object or some other thing, it is very often red. Apart from that, I also like the colors of precious stones. I like turquoise very much, and mixtures of reds with blue.

What are your favorite materials?

Probably painted or gilded wood . . . natural materials, lacquered objects, or decorative paintwork. I also like ceramics and materials with a cracked surface. In my designs for interior decoration objects, I have used eggshell; I wanted a rather neutral color to place the emphasis more on texture.

If you were an era, which would you be?
Now.

If you were a painting, which would you be?

Le Jardin de la Méditerranée
by Balthus.

If you were a piece of music?

"Satisfaction" by the Rolling Stones.

Do fabrics play an important part in your interior decoration? How do you use them?

I like cotton, velvet, and all handmade fabrics: kilims, blankets from the Atlas mountains. And I also have a weakness for bayadere—I'd put it everywhere!

In fashion, a cut of the scissors or a seam is of crucial importance. What aspects are most important in interior decoration?

Candlelight brings a lot of romance to a place. Aside from that, I like surprises, things that clash, are unexpected, break unity, disrupt monotony—modern paintings with Louis XV furniture, for example. Mixtures of different periods are very interesting.

As a fashion designer, what you create differs according to the season. Does this encourage you to change the décor of your house often?

I move furniture about, but there is nothing radical about the changes I make. In fashion, too, I don't think one changes style completely. There is however a common base to collections; there is no total renewal each time, otherwise it would be impossible to describe a designer's style.

What sort of atmosphere do you like to create in a house?

I appreciate comfort, joie de vivre, conviviality, and the warmth that a place can convey.

Which is your favorite room at home?

Seated on my sofa by the enormous window, I dominate the entire space, and the light is magnificent.

What small everyday pleasures does your home give you?

My daily pleasure consists chiefly of parties. I entertain my friends and family very often; it is very pleasant to meet all together at home.

Do you have a motto in interior decoration?

To remain true to oneself.

Is decorating a house the same as clothing a body?

No, because I don't feel I am an interior designer. My décor is less studied than my fashion designs. ■

If you were a house, what would you be?
A house on top of a hill in Italy.

If you were an item of furniture?
A romantic daybed.

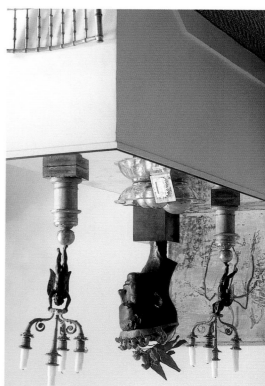

Martin Grant

In a historic district in the heart of Paris, Australian designer Martin Grant has created a small hanging garden where, only a few meters from the city's bustle, he cultivates a refined, restful way of living. The décor of his apartment displays the same discreet elegance as his collections, an endless source of inspiration.

If you were an era, what would you be?
The 1960s.

If you were an item of furniture, what would you be?
An armchair.

Where did you acquire your taste for interior decoration?

I have always collected round and ovoid objects. . . . I think my taste for interior decoration draws on very diverse elements, but first and foremost among these are my family roots. My parents and my grandmother liked very different styles. My parents' taste was more for the 1950s, 1960s, and 1970s, whereas my grandmother appreciated the nineteenth century, as well as the 1920s and 1930s. My parents liked the Scandinavian style—rather pure. Their Melbourne house, built during the 1950s, was modified around 1970 to incorporate pure spaces, many windows, and a great deal of light.

If you were a painting, what would you be?
A fifteenth-century court portrait.

Are your sources of inspiration the same both for fashion and interior decoration?

They are indeed quite close, but the décor of my apartment is less pure than the garments I design, probably because I lack space, given the number of objects I have in my home. I often use the objects I possess for my collections: There are countless little things in boxes and drawers. I take out what seems appropriate for a given season, and this sometimes becomes a source of inspiration.

Are you interested in architecture? Who is your favorite architect?

I like architecture very much, but I am not a specialist in this area. I like Frank Lloyd Wright and Tadao Ando. I have a weakness for pure shapes and lines. That aside, I am particularly fond of fifteenth-century architecture.

What is your favorite decorative style?

I like it when everything is mixed up together. A single style on its own always feels too cold, austere, or clinical. I prefer to mix the things that I pick up by browsing around: African benches, [Eero] Saarinen tables . . . often in natural materials and with sculpturesque shapes. I like primitive, rather unpolished art.

What are your favorite color combinations in interior design? Are they the same as those you use in fashion?

They are often rather unfashionable colors, a bit out of date, and rarely very light colors . . . except for red, which sometimes appears in my collections. At home I have a very bright red painting and a few other red elements that echo it. There are few colors in my apartment; it is quite neutral, and I like this neutrality, because in my work—it's true, I do not work much with color—I prefer to keep this neutral palette, in order to keep my mind free to concentrate on shapes.

What are your favorite materials?

For the house, wood—oak. I like the color of oak; the flooring in Parisian apartments inspires me.

Do fabrics play an important part in your interior decoration? How do you use them?

Do you know the saying "Cobblers always wear the worst shoes"? . . . I have a stock of fabrics in my office and I always tell myself that they would be perfect for curtains, but I never have the time, so I keep the linen curtains.

In fashion, a cut of the scissors or a seam is of crucial importance. What aspects are most important in interior decoration?

There are so many things to think about! But more than anything else, light is very important for me. I like the very subdued light in the evening, from candles—soft and warm.

If you were a house, what would you be?

*A house built in the 1960s,
very uncluttered and geometric,
or a fifteenth-century house
with a big garden.*

As a fashion designer, what you create differs according to the season. Does this encourage you to change the décor of your house often?

I like very much to move furniture around, change the arrangement, turn themes upside down. I have a small stock of objects in the cellar, and sometimes I take some out. This might begin with a color: I introduce a color and then remove others that don't go with it, so and I create a new ambiance.

What sort of atmosphere do you like to create in a house?

One of conviviality and interest. It is important to me that it should not be aseptic, that everything should not be perfectly tidy. . . . I like people to be at their ease, that there should be a feeling of life in the house. I like to entertain.

Which is your favorite room at home?

I like the living room. In general, the room that attracts me most is the one with the fireplace. It's a personal thing. . . . At my parents' house and at my grandmother's, there was a fireplace and that was where I liked to be, in the warmth with this lovely light. There is something special about fireplaces; you can look at the fire for hours.

What small everyday pleasures does your home give you?

The terrace is a veritable place of pleasure, and the gardens are another passion of mine. I love to work in a garden; it makes me happy. It's partly for this reason that I've stayed in this apartment: It is so rare to find a terrace! Also, for me, it's a pleasure to go on the terrace in the morning and sit there when the weather is good. All my plants are there in their pots—there is endless variety. I like boxwood, because it is green all year round. I have lavender, rosemary, and laurel, which I use in my cooking. To be able to do this in Paris is to feel a little as if one were in the country.

Do you have a motto in interior decoration?
No "total look," as in fashion. Interior decoration is something personal, not created for someone else. Otherwise it feels too cold. I like to grasp people's personalities through their houses.

Is decorating a house the same as clothing a body?
It's a bit different, but it's the same concept. I think I have the same approach. I'd say it's rather like designing a collection: You have different elements and you make them work together while preserving their specificity. There must be coherence, but also variety. ∎

If you were a color, what would you be?

*All blues, and especially navy blue,
powder blue, and peacock blue.*

Betsey
Johnson

The designer Betsey Johnson was first noticed during the 1960s by the rock group The Velvet Underground; since then, she has brightened American fashion with her joyous eccentricity through her floral dresses, which are very feminine. Faithful to herself, an eternal woman-child, she has made her New York apartment into a cozy nest, curled up in a pink, sugary cocoon.

If you were an era, what would you be?
The American Victorian period.

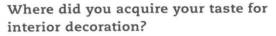

Where did you acquire your taste for interior decoration?

Decorating a house is, for me, a means of expression just as much as fashion is. I like to put different parts of my personality into it. Whether it is glamour and ultrafemininity or rock 'n' roll, it's me. I truly believe that each thing one likes is part of a whole. My apartment is the only place where I really do what I want; I can express myself without the constraints of my work. I don't have to sell anything: It's 100 percent me, without any restrictions.

Are your sources of inspiration the same both for fashion and interior decoration?

The things that inspire me are always more or less the same ones. I adore collecting small objects or portraits and sculptures of women, and I like browsing in antique shops, or second-hand shops where I can also find old clothes, small baby-doll tunics that can help me also in my collections. Whether it is for my garments or for my home, there are common denominators, such as colors that I adore. My inspiration for this apartment was the writer Dorothy Parker, and a certain decadent vision of Hollywood. Also, since I travel a lot, I wanted it to feel a bit like a hotel here, with very little maintenance—easy to live in.

Are you interested in architecture? Who is your favorite architect?

When I had my house in Mexico built, I went to study the arches and vaulting of cathedrals to seek inspiration. The result—the architecture of my house—was not what I had expected, and in the end it has been a disappointment. I prefer to deal with interior decoration.

What is your favorite decorative style?

I like the ambiance of small cottages, because I feel ill at ease in places that are too spacious. That aside, I do not prefer any particular style: I enjoy mixing genres. I buy objects that I like, and the period matters little. But I always prefer originals to copies.

What are your favorite color combinations in interior design? Are they the same as those you use in fashion?

There is a lot of energy in bright colors, and those are the ones I use most in my designs and in my houses. Strong, luminous colors are reinvigorating. When I decorated this apartment, I did not want to use pink because it is completely tied up with my work . . . but this color is part of me and I came back to it entirely naturally—or perhaps it came back to me. I heard recently that it is psychologically very beneficial: I agree entirely!

What are your favorite materials?

Very natural, unrefined, or cold materials bore me . . . apart from that, there are no specific materials with which I decorate my rooms.

If you were a painting, what would you be?
An Odalisque *by Matisse.*

If you were a fabric, what would you be?

A magnificent chintz with a floral print.

If you were a house, what would you be?

A doll's house.

Do fabrics play an important part in your interior decoration? How do you use them?

Fabrics are at the very root of my interior decoration; I can't live without fabrics, and they are more or less the same as I use for my garments. I love them silky, very feminine, brightly colored—with a slightly worn, aged feel to them, and often they are floral.

In fashion, a cut of the scissors or a seam is of crucial importance. What aspects are most important in interior decoration?

In my work I have always paid a great deal of attention to details, even if they are hidden. . . . I remember that when I began to create my collections I designed a very simple little T-shirt dress, but I had put some pretty little buttons on the front, which opened on a very delicate floral print. Details are that little bit extra that makes an enormous difference. In my décor, the many objects that I collect are positioned in very specific places, and I immediately know if someone has moved them. They are important to me; they tell my story, and say who I am. The bunches of roses that I place everywhere are also part of these essential details.

As a fashion designer, what you create differs according to the season. Does this encourage you to change the décor of your houses often?

Color is probably the thing I change most easily. For example, before it was pink, my apartment used to be mostly in fairly bright yellow shades, with floral curtains. It was very pretty! If I had to change again, I would like to put up wallpaper with lovely flowers.

What sort of atmosphere do you like to create in a house?

I want the atmosphere to resemble me as much as possible. Since I live alone, I like my objects, my little possessions, to amuse me . . . and also I must above all live in a very cozy place.

Which is your favorite place at home?

I love settling down on my sofa and watching an old film on television, or drawing for hours. I often fall asleep there, too!

What small everyday pleasures does your home give you?

When I come home in the evening, I feel good when everything is in its place. I look at the photographs of my daughter and granddaughter in their frames, and that soothes me.

Do you have a motto in interior decoration?

I have no motto.

Is decorating a house the same as clothing a body?

The action is almost the same. I earned my first money dressing a chair! A very well-known furniture company had organized a competition asking several fashion designers to dress one of their pieces of furniture. I chose a chair with rounded lines that reminded me of a woman's body. I dressed it in a feminine way, with a skirt that reached the floor. ∎

If you were a piece of music, what would you be?

A good rock 'n' roll tune.

José Lévy

Appreciated in the world of men's fashion for his precise, slightly off-beat creations, José Lévy tackles interior design with the same sense of excitement and feeling for detail. In his bright Haussmann-style apartment in Paris, the gentle poetry of his furnishings overturns conventions of subtlety and refinement.

If you were an era, what would you be?
The present day.

If you were an item of furniture, what would you be?
A broad, comfortable sofa.

Where did you acquire your taste for interior decoration?

I think it comes from my interest in people, objects, and encounters with others . . . in what goes on the body and is around the body. It is part of the same thing. I am very inquisitive; I love going to the flea market and walking around, browsing in the second-hand and antique shops. When I travel, I always poke about in the markets and shops to try to understand how people live their everyday lives.

There is an unaffected side to my idea of interior decoration. I like it to be visible, but it must not interfere with life. For me, comfort is a very important notion, both for clothes and for a house . . . a very good bed, or a very good sofa, must not only be handsome but also pleasant. Similarly, there are two ways of feeling comfortable in a garment: It has to do with taste, but also with the body. The two—aesthetics and comfort—must balance each other.

Are your sources of inspiration the same both for fashion and interior decoration?

My chief source is Paris, all the different sides of Paris, from the tourist cliché to the most sophisticated, unsettling aspects.

My apartment is a prime example: very elaborate moldings, glazed flooring, a fireplace, perfect harmony between the very bright rooms—in short, an "efficient middle-class" world, absolutely present and neutral at the same time.

But there is also nature, greenery, flowers: I like the contrast between nature and the city (as in the Luxembourg Gardens). I always have greenery at home, even if it is only "imported" greenery. I admire the botanist Patrick Blanc: The luxuriant, organic, and strange sides to his work inspire me immensely. My travels and my rather distant country house—in Marrakech—are also sources of inspiration.

Are you interested in architecture? Who is your favorite architect?

I respond to architecture, but my interest doesn't go beyond that. What I like is the emotion that a place can produce, the way it comes to life. There are some very beautiful architectural structures that are absolutely sublime but lifeless.

What is your favorite decorative style?

I like the idea of a marriage between this Parisian setting and French-style decorative arts, but of course this would be supported by lots of other things . . . travel, for example, even though I am not crazy about ethnic artifacts in Paris.

As far as furniture goes, I quite like the 1930s and 1940s, as well as contemporary things. I am quite attracted by the twentieth century in general, because otherwise I feel that the pulse of life is too far removed from me. I need to feel a more or less immediate connection with things. I like antique shops and second-hand shops, but I also acknowledge that IKEA can offer a way in to design at very accessible prices. I believe more in the aesthetics of taste than in those of money.

What are your favorite color combinations in interior design? Are they the same as those you use in fashion?

I play with colors a lot, but I don't have a favorite . . . rather, there are interplays between different colors: a lot of monochrome and at the same time rather violent colors. As in fashion, I use colors instinctively. I play with blues, harmonies of off-white shades, and colors that are not always obvious. I like it when a shadow brings a filter of color onto walls and then, suddenly, the colors change, evolve.

What are your favorite materials?

I really like porcelain, mercury glass, and wood, but also plastic. It depends on the object in question, in fact. I like mirrors because of the light they reflect back. I am quite demanding where light is concerned . . . I could not live in a dark place. Sometimes I change the lighting in places I go to. You can ruin a beautiful place with an unflattering light, which doesn't throw the space into relief. Conversely, one can make a simple place wonderful with really pretty light. It really plays a part in the atmosphere of a place.

If you were a color, what would you be?
Very dark navy blue—blue-black.

If you were a fabric?
A Milano weave, very tightly woven, both soft and taut.

Do fabrics play an important part in your interior decoration? How do you use them?
Not at all. I don't get excited about fabrics in my home.

In fashion, a cut of the scissors or a seam is of crucial importance. What aspects are most important in interior decoration?
I give special importance to the way objects complement each other in my home. I like hidden details, when a lot is going on all over the place but you don't notice it at first sight. I find objects and then I place them vary carefully, but they must fit in completely naturally, and a touch casually.

As a fashion designer, what you create differs according to the season. Does this encourage you to change the décor of your houses often?
As far as form is concerned, I need regular renewal. By contrast, regarding background change is much slower, more thoughtful.

It is initially an interior evolution. . . . I do not change personality every six months: It develops over time, matures, fills out—I hope. This influences my way of living, of working, of managing my inner life, but also my relations with others. . . . This evolution spreads out into my work and my private life.

If you were a piece of music, what would you be?

Something by Erik Satie.

What sort of atmosphere do you like to create in a house?
One of comfort, intimacy, without ostentation.

Which is your favorite room at home?
In this apartment, I like all the rooms.
In general, I feel comfortable in kitchens, even though mine is not very big.

What small everyday pleasures does your home give you?
Getting up in the morning in a place I like, hearing the twittering of the birds, and the view from my bedroom, with the ivy climbing up the wall of the nearby building.

Do you have a motto in interior decoration?
No. Rather, I apply small principles that grow out of what I like and dislike.

Is decorating a house the same as clothing a body?
For me, this is like an extension. What you put on your body is what touches you and governs how you appear to others. This has something to do with intimacy. Because of this, there are more constraints, more thinking, more fears. An interior says something about you, it also portrays you, but it does not touch you physically: It is next to you, not on you. So you feel freer; you can show things that you would not show on your own body. ■

If you were a painting, what would you be?
One by John Currin.

A house?
My own house or my apartment.

Christian Louboutin

Creator of the celebrated red-soled shoes—veritable objects of desire for the world's elegant women—Christian Louboutin satisfies his natural curiosity by making many journeys around the planet. His Parisian apartment exudes an Oriental fragrance that calls to mind his passion for Egypt.

If you were a color, what would you be?

The red of my shoes.

Where did you acquire your taste for interior decoration?

I am curious, first and foremost. My taste for interior decoration did not come from fashion at all, but it seems to me to be a natural extension when one is working in a sphere where aesthetics play a part . . . a continuity that extends as far as the décor in one's apartment. I have always liked possessing things that I can look at. I have a love of objects. My father was a cabinet-maker; he made things out of wood. I must have been influenced by this, for I love craftsmanship in wood. Since the age of twelve I have collected shoes, clothes, and objects.

Are your sources of inspiration the same both for fashion and interior decoration?

In a way I am defined by this. There is no separation between my professional life and my working life. I decorated my first shop with materials and objects that I had at home. The objects I possess come and go. This is an advantage when one has several places. It is like a treasure chest. I am not a collector, but a lover of things who amasses them.

Are you interested in architecture? Who is your favorite architect?

I adore [Luis] Barragán and Egyptian architecture. Their work contains very powerful shadows and exaggerated angles and depths of recesses that bring to mind the drawings of [Giorgio] De Chirico. The architect's profession is a fascinating and impressive one, with all the responsibilities it carries.

If you were a painting, what would you be?
A poster for Adventures of
Tintin: Land of Black Gold.

What is your favorite decorative style?

This changes, actually. I know the 1920s and 1940s, the style of the eighteenth century, and that of the turn of the twentieth fairly well. I also like the Byzantine period. I go in phases mostly, a bit like fashion. There are times when certain periods or genres are more or less popular. In fashion, the 1950s are an almost perfect period in terms of the quality of shapes, of lines.

I have a great fondness for the Directoire, in painting, clothes, architecture, and furniture. The Vérot-Dodat Gallery in Paris represents everything I love.

I own a house in Egypt, and I like Egyptian-style settings in interior decoration, but I would not like an interior that was a reconstruction—this gives an impersonal atmosphere. Unless one is a specialist in a given period, I see no point in confining oneself to a single style.

What are your favorite color combinations in interior design? Are they the same as those you use in fashion?

I like deep ochres with dark reds. It's rather Directoire or Empire style. I also like violet with green, which I use a great deal for my shoes—chartreuse and purple. It is inspiration that comes from the countryside, from plants and flowers.

What are your favorite materials?

Wood, brass, and bronze.

Do fabrics play an important part in your interior decoration? How do you use them?

I use a lot of Suzani, Uzbek, and Ottoman fabrics, to cover furniture completely or to hang on the walls. I love velvet, but in small quantities, because it is strongly associated with winter.

In fashion, a cut of the scissors or a seam is of crucial importance. What aspects are most important in interior decoration?

Curtains, probably, even though I find that these are the hardest thing to do: You have to watch how the light filters through them. I had some curtains made in costume cloth and in the fabric used for the back of men's waistcoats.

If you were a house, what would you be?
A mud house in Egypt.

If you were an item of furniture, what would you be?

A bed, or a mattress.

If you were an era?

The Byzantine period.

As a fashion designer, what you create differs according to the season. Does this encourage you to change the décor of your houses often?

I don't actually spend enough time at home and I'm not organized enough. It is more a case of objects being moved about.

What sort of atmosphere do you like to create in a house?

The only things I don't like are empty interiors and interiors that are too technical, where the most important place is occupied by the stereo or the television.

Which is your favorite room at home?

The bedroom: not because of the décor but because I love sleeping. I love my bed. I see bedrooms as boxes. I like the idea that the bedroom should be really small, and contain few things.

What small everyday pleasures does your home give you?

Being in the heart of Paris, feeling that I am in town. I have a very Parisian view, with an apartment building opposite my place, a café, and some prostitutes. It's very urban; I like it.

Do you have a motto in interior decoration?

None, apart from "no wallpaper."

Is decorating a house the same as clothing a body?

I do not have the sense of volume with a place, but there is indeed the same idea of the importance of details. A detail can change how you see a place. A shoe is a shape, first and foremost: If its structure is good, it can be enriched with all manner of details. ■

Catherine
Malandrino

Established in New York, where she has created her own label, Catherine Malandrino personifies both the French romantic spirit and the dynamism of New York. Her urban, feminine, colorful designs emphasize the contrasts she likes, and this extends to her Manhattan apartment. Yellows and reds gaily answer each other, like a connecting thread, in this place that is constantly evolving.

If you were a color, what would you be?
Lemon yellow.

If you were a painting, what would you be?

A blue canvas by Yves Klein, which is both very powerful and also leaves all the space for my imagination.

Where did you acquire your taste for interior decoration?

I don't use the term "interior decoration." I would describe it, rather, as an art of living, a style that can be adapted to the house, clothing, accessories, personal tastes. . . . It is a lifestyle that is found in the interior and exterior; it is a matter of finding harmony among being, appearing, and experience. When I enter an apartment, I do not ask myself how I will furnish it, but rather how I will live there, how we will live together, what we will share, and how. It is really a question more of lifestyle than of interior decoration.

Are your sources of inspiration the same both for fashion and interior decoration?

I try, above all, to create environments that are first and foremost visually attractive, by creating open spaces with high ceilings and views. Next, I think it is important to find the important spot in a space. Since I attach great importance to documentation in my work and in my life, the library is a central element, whereas the kitchen matters little, because I do not cook much. It is more like a corridor where I do not linger long, and must open onto the dining and living rooms. I pay a lot of attention to the places where my family and friends meet: around the sofa, or around the table. Then, I clear up the space: Whatever is too "furnished" bothers me. With clothes, I work in the same way. I go for the essentials, first creating a shape, a structure, proportions, before going into detail. This is my guiding principle in fashion and in the home.

Are you interested in architecture? Who is your favorite architect?

I find Oscar Niemeyer very inspiring; I like the feminine curves of his creations. They inspire me, and they are always in my head.

What is your favorite decorative style?

Above all, I am sensitive to solid shapes. As for style, I tend to prefer fairly pure places, but I like eclecticism. By that I mean that the general features and atmosphere are largely inspired by the 1960s, but that does not prevent the addition of, for example, pieces of African origin. I like my home to arouse my curiosity: It is a place of inspiration and a place for living. I have a stuffed bird at home. It isn't just an object: What interests me is what it represents for me in terms of texture and color. I need this eclecticism, and I do not confine myself to a period; I blend periods and genres.

What are your favorite color combinations in interior design? Are they the same as those you use in fashion?

They are always quite similar: There is always a rather strong dominant color, around which the collection, or the apartment, is put together. There are two main colors in my home. There is citrus yellow, which is developed into a broad palette from yellow-green to absinthe via lemon yellow. This color is also part of my collections and it is always around me, even though I do not always wear it: It is a recurrent color. I like to contrast this with pure red; it is a source of energy. I like this duality of colors in my collections, too. I can be minimalist with lines, but never with colors. I like atmospheres that are made vibrant by the contrasts between colors. This applies in all the rooms in my house, like a connecting thread.

What are your favorite materials?

It is more the contrast between materials that interests me: wood in a matte finish, a wardrobe in red lacquer, a transparent table by Christophe Pillet that reflects light.

Do fabrics play an important part in your interior decoration? How do you use them?

Fabrics are important for their texture. Here, too, I play with contrasts between materials, both in my collections and in my house. My sofa is in a thick, deep red canvas, the ottomans are in terry wool, the bedclothes in Egyptian cotton. On the other hand, I like to leave windows bare, or just fitted with blinds, to leave the view as open as possible. I like household linen, and I attach great importance to table napkins and towels in very bright colors; I find that fabrics are a good way to renew one's interior.

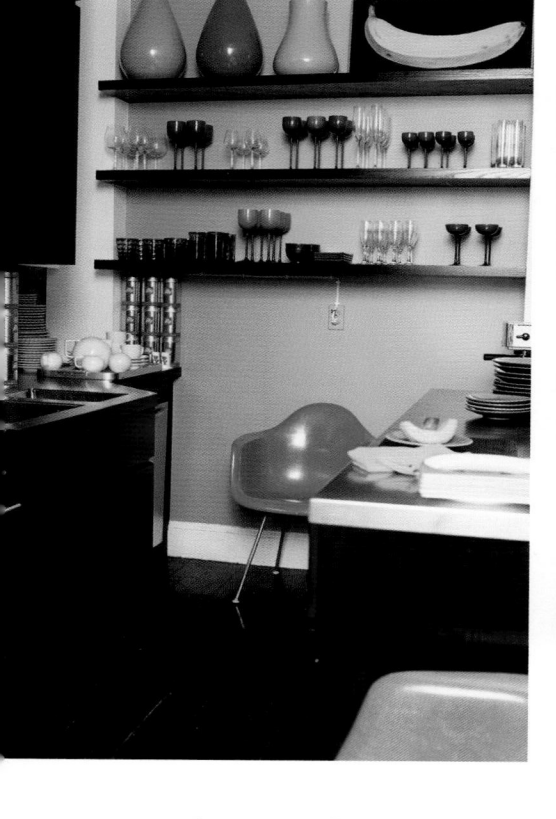

If you were a house, what would you be?

The Fondation Maeght in Saint-Paul-de-Vence.

In fashion, a cut of the scissors or a seam is of crucial importance. What aspects are most important in interior decoration?

The way a table is laid also reflects style. I like oversized plates, which enhance the appearance of food, and fine silverware. Also, I like to drink wine from very beautiful glasses, such as those from Murano, which I collect. The dinner table is very important to me: It is a time for sharing.

As a fashion designer, what you create differs according to the season. Does this encourage you to change the décor of your house often?

In my house everything is free, and nothing is fixed. No painting is attached to a wall; everything is simply placed where it is. A painting will be moved from the living room to the bathroom, the glasses in the kitchen will go into the living room. I like spaces that are built around how objects are chosen and placed. As in my collections, I never make drastic changes. It is a style that is being formed, work that is always evolving.

What sort of atmosphere do you like to create in a house?

I like convivial atmospheres, a place where one wants to stay, where one feels good, with this idea of comfort. On the other hand, I like to leave space for freedom of movement and for each person's personality to express itself. I have a horror of overcrowded spaces; instead, everything must be light, with places for self-expression.

Which is your favorite room at home?

It is certainly the living room, which is a combined drawing room, kitchen, and dining room, where we all spend most of our time together.

What small everyday pleasures does your home give you?

I love having coffee early in the morning, at sunrise. It is a moment when the family are together, a shared moment that I would not miss for anything in the world.

Do you have a motto in interior decoration?

An apartment is a place of inspiration, and for that one must not be afraid to take risks and be adventurous, because in order to be inspired one must first be able to surprise oneself.

If you were a fabric, what would you be?

Silk muslin.

And if you were a piece of music?

"Chabadabada" by Francis Lai and Pierre Barouh.

Is decorating a house the same as clothing a body?

I am not dressing a body, because I cannot detach the body from the mind. I don't dress an empty body in the same way as I don't dress an empty apartment. Above all other things, I seek the harmony, the magic that will be created. The apartment is a way of expressing one's personality, desires, and choices, as well as being a way of forming oneself. ■

If you were an item of furniture?

A light or a dining table.

If you were an era?

Tomorrow.

Marcel
Marongiu

An admirer of pure lines and "noncolors," Marcel Marongiu shows the same preferences in his personal world and in his interior design. When, in the Norman countryside, he allowed his Swedish background a free rein, the interplay of whites, grays, and blacks brought a theatrical note here and there to the Gustavian rigor.

If you were an era, what would you be?
The eighteenth century.

If you were a fabric, what would you be?
Linen.

Where did you acquire your taste for interior decoration?

It comes from the same need as my taste for fashion. It is probably, from my earliest childhood, a deep desire to take refuge in creativity itself, in a world I have created myself. This started with painting; then came fashion and interior decoration. There is no limit to creativity. I have shaped a world in order to surround myself with an environment in which I feel good.

Are you interested in architecture? Who is your favorite architect?

Very much so, and there are many architects I like. Étienne Louis Boulais, an eighteenth-century architect, built virtually nothing; because of the Revolution, his projects never saw the light of day. However, he had some absolutely astonishing ideas, very avant-garde for the time. . . . Also, I would mention some American architects such as Richard Neutra and [Pierre] Koenig, who play with the use of space and the way it contrasts with nature, while at the same time paying it great respect. In this sense, they are perhaps the forerunners of Minimalism and of that avant-gardism whose creations interact with nature.

Are your sources of inspiration the same both for fashion and interior decoration?

They have the same foundations, more or less. In fashion, what matters is the outline and the way things are put together. The same applies in decoration: I give priority to materials, which I allow to express themselves, and after that I stifle them as little as possible, whether we are talking about wood, a color, or a handsome eighteenth-century gilded mirror.

In fashion, a perfectly constructed dress can be left in plain black as long as it has the right construction, the right shapes . . . and the person inside does the rest.

Interior decoration must not stifle the people who live in it. For me, the setting is always in equilibrium, in harmony with the people who live with it.

If you were an item of furniture?
An old leather armchair.

If you were a house, what would you be?
A Flemish manor house.

What is your favorite decorative style?

I developed my own sensibility in the way I mix things together. I am not fixed in any one period: A single style makes you paralyzed, historical, dated. I think every world is a personal one. Each of us must associate, combine things. For my part, it is a mixture of eighteenth century, the Nordic style of the 1950s and 1960s, Scandinavian design, and a little touch of the ethnic, often from North Africa and India. I try to fit these elements together. I have this penchant for the eighteenth century because it was a time when people went very far in expressing themselves; there wasn't this bourgeois morality of the nineteenth century.

What are your favorite color combinations in interior design? Are they the same as those you use in fashion?

The basic palette is always the same: black, gray, white, beige, sand—which go with almost everything and enhance what I add afterward. For example, a gray wall with a wooden table, to allow the latter all the space to express itself. In fashion, it's the same: Always leave a small opening through which the person can express themselves.

What are your favorite materials?

I like old wood or wood that has acquired a patina through time, together with silver: a very natural, unvarnished side combined with a refined touch, but one that ages with the years. Always, this idea of time.

Do fabrics play an important part in your interior decoration? How do you use them?

Since I work with fabrics all day long, I don't feel like having too many at home. The fabric I like best is linen, because it is a material that ages wonderfully.

Linen lives and changes texture; very stiff at first, it softens with time. Also, it always has little imperfections, which I especially like.

In fashion, the details of the way a garment is cut, or a piece of embroidery, are crucial; in interior design, to which details do you give priority?

I don't see either fashion or interior decoration in that way. It is the whole that is fundamentally important. But, since the whole is made up of details, I shall go into detail. . . . Lighting, for example, is very important for me. A lovely place can be utterly ruined by disastrous lighting. In the evening, I love to have only candles. . . . I try to re-create the atmosphere of the film *Barry Lyndon.*

If you were a painting, what would you be?

A painting by Robert Motherwell.

As a fashion designer, what you create differs according to the season. Does this encourage you to change the décor of your house often?

Not necessarily, and it's a bit like that in fashion, too. I proclaim a very specific style that asserts itself from one collection to the next: It's not a case of change for its own sake, but rather continuity through change. A human being does not change from one season to another.

He or she has his or her own style, a particular way of being and living. I am interested in people who see life as a continuum. We build ourselves up, little by little. On the other hand, I don't like to live statically, and even though my tastes are constant, I am happy to evolve within that framework.

What sort of atmosphere do you like to create in a house?

If I must put that in a nutshell, let's say warm and nostalgic. I am very fond of the Gustavian style of the late eighteenth century, in Sweden, where everything tends to be white or pale gray, with a lot of patina. Because the kingdom of Sweden was so poor, it was not possible to use gilt. Everything was painted in oil paint, which soon acquired a patina. The means of expression were thus found through the form: Perhaps that is how the Scandinavian language, in which what matters are the essentials, was born. It is the form that touches me.

Which is your favorite room at home?

The living room, because it is black and white, reduced to its essentials. The materials convey something, the doors have a patina, and there are great flat areas of white and black. I need this purity and this visual simplicity around me to feel at ease.

What small everyday pleasures does your home give you?

Cooking, going to the market, having my friends around me in the kitchen when I cook up my dishes, and drinking a good glass of wine with them. We talk. . . . Here, I spend time with my friends, I rediscover the family atmosphere I had when I was little. . . . I share day-to-day life with people I love.

Do you have a motto in interior decoration?

Let objects express themselves.

Is decorating a house the same as clothing a body?

It is quite similar, in fact. I make a shell so that the person feels good, fits within the garment, or within the place. When I dress a body, it is to make this person more beautiful, taller, younger. . . . It's cheating a bit, thanks to the garment, so that she feels more attractive. With a house, I try to make it warm to welcome people. ∎

If you were a color, what would you be?

Gray.

Gilles
Mendel

A worthy heir to the furrier J. Mendel, established in New York for many years, Gilles Mendel lends his signature to a showy ready-to-wear line whose sumptuous evening gowns flaunt subtle details of airy fur. His apartment, near Central Park, displays a pure luxury in which small touches of red heighten with ardor a black-and-white setting.

If you were a painting, what would you be?
*One by [Albert-Ernest]
Carrier-Belleuse.*

If you were an item of furniture, what would you be?
A comfortable armchair.

A house?
One by Frank Lloyd Wright.

■ **If you were a fabric, what would you be?**
Silk.

Where did you acquire your taste for interior decoration?

I come from a family who adores art, and I was fortunate enough to be able to appreciate beautiful things since my childhood. It is important—even essential—for me to live in an environment that is in keeping with my designs. It is a general view of life and the pleasure of being surrounded by a pleasant atmosphere, a reflection of the personality.

Are your sources of inspiration the same both for fashion and interior decoration?

In a way, they are almost the same sources of inspiration. I am very fond of the chic, modern 1970s, which can be seen in my apartment. Fashion changes the whole time; interior decoration cannot change every minute. At present, I design four collections per year, and each collection is a complete renewal of certain aesthetic ideas. I design for elegant women; I like luxury, and when I go home I need to see a place that is identical to this aestheticism I have in fashion. On the other hand, I prefer to live in a more minimalist, bare, and simple space than the dresses and furs I design.

Are you interested in architecture? Who is your favorite architect?

I like modernism very much, but with a reference to the past. I like the work of Richard Meier and also that of Eero Saarinen, who creates a perfect balance between the nobility of materials and shapes that are often curved and feminine. I am very inspired by his architecture for the TWA air terminal [at Kennedy Airport] in New York, dating from the 1960s, and his furniture, such as the table in my dining room.

What is your favorite decorative style?

I spent my entire childhood surrounded by Art Deco interior decoration—my mother was a great collector—and I am very fond of it for sentimental reasons. However, when I arrived in New York, I wanted to break away from this style. The interior decoration I like tends to have a neutral foundation—black or white—like a painter's canvas, onto which I bring touches of color or the shapes of objects I like. It is like a Mondrian, where the few colors stand out against the background. I believe it is objects that create the style; they contrast with the neutral walls. When one is lucky enough to have an aesthetically pleasing architectural space, I also like a certain bareness.

What are your favorite color combinations in interior design? Are they the same as those you use in fashion?

In fashion, I love pale colors, which are very sophisticated. Only rarely do I use very bright colors, or even black or white. At home, it is the opposite. Black and white allow me to add objects with color, such as red, which is all over the place here: in a lamp or a piece of Chinese furniture, in a carpet, or even a candle. Red is very sensual.

What are your favorite materials?

I am very attracted to noble materials, such as fur for covering an armchair, or black marble and floors in dark wood, for example. Or there could be surprising mixtures, such as Plexiglas with leather and mirrors—very Halston!

Do fabrics play an important part in your interior decoration? How do you use them?

I love the combination of matte with glossy fabrics, or of rich, winter material with simpler, more summery fabrics. I like mixtures and contrasts. My sofa is in coarse linen, but the cushions placed on it are silk and fur. In fashion, I work in the same way: For a summer collection, I designed a very light silk coat, to which I added white mink on the bottom and back. It is positioned in such a way that the fur takes on a light, summery quality.

If you were a color, what would you be?

Black: both neutral and dramatic.

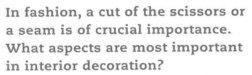

**In fashion, a cut of the scissors or
a seam is of crucial importance.
What aspects are most important
in interior decoration?**
The more bare a house is, the more details
matter: Finishes are essential, whether these
are of the paint on the walls or the floor
covering. And then light also plays a crucial
role; it is what gives a house impact.

**As a fashion designer, what you
create differs according to the
season. Does this encourage you
to change the décor of your house
often?**
I renew my apartment's interior decoration
by changing objects regularly. The foundation
remains identical.

**What sort of atmosphere do you like
to create in a house?**
Clearly, I like a cheerful, warm atmosphere in a
place that must not be overloaded, so that I can
work without being unsettled by too much
profusion around me. In the evening, I like an
intimate ambiance, which is produced by
discreet lighting, like points of light.

**Which is your favorite room at
home?**
I settle into my armchair in the corner of the
living room, with the window behind me, which
gives me a fine light for drawing.

**What small everyday pleasures does
your home give you?**
When I have a moment to myself, I love
watching old 1930s films in my living room.
I might watch several in a row. . . . They are also
a great source of inspiration for me.

**Do you have a motto in interior
decoration?**
Live surrounded by things you love!

**Is decorating a house the same as
clothing a body?**
It is indeed very similar, in that one derives
pleasure from both; it's like a fantasy. On the
other hand, while a woman can change her
clothes every day depending on her state of
mind, a house is an experience over a long
period of time, which tells the story of a
person's soul, of their life. ■

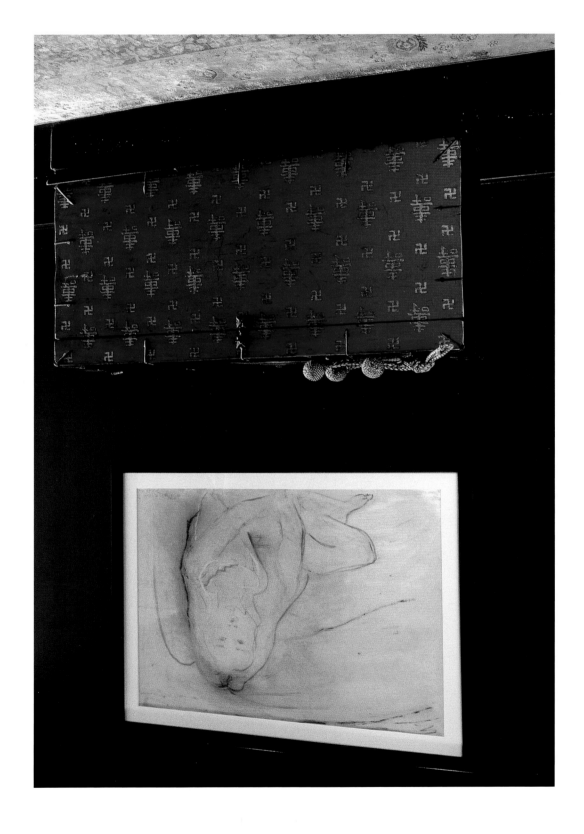

If you were a piece of music?
Jimmy Page.

Rick
Owens

Rick Owens is an American in Paris, and the designer of the label that bears his name, as well as artistic director of the celebrated French furrier Révillon. He displays the "glunge" style—the term, he explains, comes from the combination of "glamour" and "grunge"—in the interior of his home, where cashmere and fur luxuriously caress bare concrete.

If you were a fabric, what would you be?
Washed gray cashmere felt.

If you were a color, what would you be?
Gray.

A room?
The bathroom in Pierre Chareau's Maison de Verre.

Where did you acquire your taste for interior decoration?
I always hold Art Moderne and Bauhaus up as my standards for interiors and clothes—simple grace, form following function.

Are your sources of inspiration the same both for fashion and interior decoration?
I think of them both in very physical terms, the way a dress caresses a body or the way a chair cups the figure. The surface textures of both are paramount.

Are you interested in architecture? Who is your favorite architect?
I particularly like Robert Mallet-Stevens, Eileen Grey, and Herzog & de Meuron.

What is your favorite decorative style?
Jean-Michel Frank is my favorite. But then, I like Luigi Colani, too . . .

What are your favorite color combinations in interior design? Are they the same as those you use in fashion?

I cocoon myself with "dust," a soft, warm gray I've been using in my collections since day one; I always think of it as a transition color, twilight or dawn, a gentle hush of expectation. . . . And a crisp, modern iPod white.

What are your favorite materials?

Plywood, resin, bone, cashmere, glass, foam rubber, leather, and fur.

Do fabrics play an important part in your interior decoration? How do you use them?

I like to upholster pieces in my washed dust cashmere felt. It exudes a sense of quiet insulation.

In fashion, a cut of the scissors or a seam is of crucial importance. What aspects are most important in interior decoration?

Order and reason. I love looking at the warmth of personal mementos and interesting clutter, but I could never live that way; it makes me think of a teenager's room, plastered with posters. That need for reassurance is too naked for me, maybe. I like for my eyes to be able to stretch out uninterrupted.

As a fashion designer, what you create differs according to the season. Does this encourage you to change the décor of your house often?

The need to change so much strikes me as a bit frivolous—but maybe I'm just stodgy. I like big, solid furniture and a sense of permanence. I always throw away the glossy covers of new books right away. The cloth bindings are so much more beautiful—especially after they fade a bit . . . and it makes me feel that they're "home."

What sort of atmosphere do you like to create in a house?

Like there's plenty of space to spin around like crazy and not knock anything over . . . and comfortably collapse on something big . . .

If you were a painting, what would you be?
Gustave Moreau's Apparition.

If you were an item of furniture, what would you be?
A concrete bench.

Which is your favorite room at home?

I don't know if I can pick one. I'm planning on becoming obsessed with each one, one at a time.

What small everyday pleasures does your home give you?

Seeing the first wisteria blossoms in the spring and watching the birds play on the terrace. Every once in a while, they have a ceremony in the Jardin de la Ministère de la Défense, right under the terrace, and a small band and soldiers in full uniform march through and play "La Marseillaise" for a visiting dignitary. It can be unexpectedly moving.

Is decorating a house the same as clothing a body?

Same thing to me; both are about arranging pleasing proportions in relation to the body. ■

If you were a house, what would you be?
Casa Malaparte.

If you were an era, what would you be?
The 1940s.

John
Rocha

For many years, John Rocha has worked in his collections constantly to come up with new shapes using the most luxurious of materials. In his Dublin house, he displays this taste for pure lines, subtle colors, and details, with neither preciousness nor ostentation. Here, the emphasis is on light, comfort, and conviviality.

If you were a house, what would you be?
One by Le Corbusier.

If you were a color, what would you be?
Winter white or elephant gray.

A painting?
Wall of Light by Sean Scully.

Where did you acquire your taste for interior decoration?

I think all my work draws its inspiration from a combination of my life, my story, and my travels. I don't follow trends very much, but rather seek out a certain beauty of things that guides me toward my goals. My taste for interior decoration balances my desire for comfort in a spiritual and a physical sense. My fashion work is a natural progression, a development of my ideas over a given period—certain ideas take shape, develop, and can be decided upon the following season.

Are your sources of inspiration the same both for fashion and interior decoration?

I think I gave my answer in responding to the first question.

If you were an era, what would you be?

The present day.

Are you interested in architecture? Who is your favorite architect?

I am passionately interested in architecture because I am profoundly convinced that many creative disciplines are closely linked. I believe architecture is one of the great creative processes; it truly constitutes a part of our environment. I began by working on interior decoration projects, but I quickly came to understand that to create spaces that truly expressed my style it was necessary to work closely with the architects and to play an active role in the design and structure of buildings. I like many architects, past and present, particularly Tadao Ando: I greatly admire his sensitivity and his highly inspired use of hard materials such as concrete, wood, and glass.

What is your favorite decorative style?

I prefer a bright setting that I can decorate, and since I am a rather ordered person, I like tidy spaces—a fairly simple style but one with a pronounced character.

What are your favorite color combinations in interior design? Are they the same as those you use in fashion?

In interior decoration, my range of main colors is almost always based on neutral shades— off-white, the tones of wood, oyster gray, or putty. I add details inspired by my travels and my work, which bring other colors to the textures. When I design a garment, my palette of colors is always centered on black, and often includes white or cream. Depending on the season, I add other shades, most frequently dustlike colors, but I also play with more assertive colors such as reds, purples, and yellows.

What are your favorite materials?
I don't much like synthetic surfaces. I like wood and stone, oak, ebony, walnut, limestone, slate, and white marble. Glass and crystal allow light to play in interesting ways.

Do fabrics play an important part in your interior decoration? How do you use them?
Since my main interest is fashion, fabrics are also very important to me in interior decoration. I generally use plain fabrics as a base, to which I later add patterns. This translates as curtains, sofas, and armchairs in plain linen, complemented by old fabrics for cushions and rugs.

In fashion, a cut of the scissors or a seam is of crucial importance. What aspects are most important in interior decoration?
I think the most important thing in a successful interior design is the way in which space is created and defined. That aside, the essential elements are, in my view, light—both natural and artificial—and surfaces. If these two elements are present, a space will be very pleasant to live in, even if it is quite bare.

As a fashion designer, what you create differs according to the season. Does this encourage you to change the décor of your house often?
My job as a fashion designer is not driven by trends, even though design is constantly changing. Roughly the same is true of the interior decoration of my house. While the basic elements, such as choice of materials and colors, remain the same, I introduce new textiles and other paints that produce subtle changes.

If you were a piece of music, what would you be?
Reggae with a touch of country.

What sort of atmosphere do you like to create in a house?

More than anything else, I hope to create a place where the occupants feel comfortable and soothed. I like to think that a space can be relaxing and stimulating at the same time.

Which is your favorite room at home?

No question—my bathroom. I find it very pleasant to relax in my deep stone bathtub and look at the sky.

What small everyday pleasures does your home give you?

My morning bath.

Do you have a motto in interior decoration?

Not really. But as in my work in fashion, I try to create beautiful things to make people happy.

Is decorating a house the same as clothing a body?

I hope I am not just dressing bodies, but also people. I want to dress people just as I want to help them to have a pleasant place where they like to spend time. ■

If you were an item of furniture?
A chair by Norman Cherner.

Agatha Ruiz de la Prada

The flamboyant fashion designer Agatha Ruiz de la Prada, from Madrid, brings into her house a certain joie de vivre, in which light drenches the bright colors of gigantic flowers and ubiquitous heart motifs. The décor thus becomes playful and invigorating.

If you were a color, what would you be?
Fuchsia.

If you were a piece of furniture, what would you be?

A bed.

Where did you acquire your taste for interior decoration?

I come from a family of architects: My father is an architect, and my grandfather and great-grandfather were, too. I also had links with the world of architecture through the family of my maternal grandfather, who was one of Gaudí's patrons. When I was a child, we lived in a magnificent house in the heart of Madrid, one of the city's finest. My father, who was a collector of modern art, had set up his design studio, and a museum, on the top floor. At the time, no one knew about modern art, so we thought this was madness.

I feel a bit like a frustrated architect, but I have always worked in interior design . . . because I am obsessed with houses.

If you were a house?
A house by the sea.

If you were an era?
The twenty-first century.

Are you still interested in architecture?

I am quite capable of traveling many kilometers to go and see a fine house. I even began to study architecture, but it proved too difficult to combine this with my work and my children. I am friends with many architects and I love the avant-garde. I greatly admire Rem Koolhaas and Norman Foster.

Moreover, I find that fashion is getting ever closer to architecture. Many brands call on the greatest architects to create their shops or their showrooms.

Are your sources of inspiration the same both for fashion and interior decoration?

My source of inspiration has always been modern art, probably because I spent my childhood among painters. A few years ago, at an exhibition on pop art at the Beaubourg center, I realized just how much growing up during the pop art period has been an influence on my work.

What is your favorite decorative style?

I like living in my own time . . . I don't like antiques.

What are your favorite color combinations in interior design? Are they the same as those you use in fashion?

The most important thing in a house is light. For me, color is in a sense the light of a house. To live in a colored place brings great joy; beige or black décor depresses me too much. I like bright, clear colors both in fashion and in interior design. However, the choice of colors for a house depends on various parameters, such as its situation, for example. In Paris, for a Spaniard like me, there is little light; this is why I have wanted to bring many colors into this apartment.

What are your favorite materials?

When I found this Paris apartment I had just begun work on my tile collection. I really wanted to be surrounded by this material. I think it is very important for a creative person to live with what he or she creates. But each house needs different materials, depending on where it is and on the time when it is inhabited.

Do fabrics play an important part in your interior decoration? How do you use them?

Fabrics are often very classical in interior decoration: in beige, natural, unbleached colors, or brown. They are very important in a house. I like them highly colored, with or without patterns. At one time, I used a great deal of corduroy, because there is a vast choice of colors in this material. Now, I particularly like cotton fabrics.

In fashion, a cut of the scissors or a seam is of crucial importance. What aspects are most important in interior decoration?

For me, the most important thing in a house is life. Books and pictures count for a lot in my view; they bring a house to life.

As a fashion designer, what you create differs according to the season. Does this encourage you to change the décor of your house often?

I don't like fixed things. I believe the décor of one's house should be changed regularly. I like to change the furniture in my house often.

What sort of atmosphere do you like to create in a house?

Above all, I like gaiety.

Which is your favorite room at home?

The place I prefer above all others at home is my bed, because I like to spend a lot of time there reading.

What small everyday pleasures does your home give you?

This apartment is a very intimate place for me. It is not a place where I receive many guests. Sometimes, though, friends who know how to cook—which I absolutely don't—come to my place and we dine in front of an open fire. It's wonderful!

Do you have a motto in interior decoration?

I don't have a motto, only a great love for the contemporary and for gaiety.

Is decorating a house the same as clothing a body?

I like to mix things in fashion and interior design, combining recent creations with older ones. And then, from time to time, it is necessary to purge things. In fact, there is no inconsistency between my fashion, my interior decoration, and my character. ■

If you were a painting, what would you be?
A painting by Rothko.

A fabric?
An environmentally friendly, colorful one.

Elie
Saab

A prolific and perfectionist couturier, Elie Saab transcends Hollywood glamour with his silky, ultrafeminine dresses. He is passionate about architecture, and in his house in the Lebanese mountains, he expresses his fondness for vast, airy spaces and clean lines, bathed in light.

If you were a fabric, what would you be?
Silk muslin.

If you were a house, what would you be?
My childhood home.

Where did you acquire your taste for interior decoration?

I believe that if I had not become a couturier I would have been an architect. I am very fond of the architecture of things: I like beautiful walls, facades, and spaces. I think architecture is more important than decoration. For twenty years I have never been without some building work in progress; I get great pleasure from building sites. They entertain me.

Are your sources of inspiration the same both for fashion and interior decoration?

In general, I create my houses in a style that fits in with where they are. But for the last ten years, I have preferred to live in a purified atmosphere. I don't much like houses that are too "decorated"; what I like are the shapes, dimensions, and spaces of a place.

Who is your favorite architect?

I have a very soft spot for the creations of the architect Tadao Ando, and I like the spaces created by Frank Lloyd Wright.

What is your favorite decorative style?

Before the style come people's personalities. When I go to visit friends, even if their interior decoration style is not my favorite, I appreciate that it is a reflection of their personalities. In that sense, I admire all styles, but I like it best when I can see the character, mentality, and style of a person in their house. In my own home, I like classic, timeless things.

What are your favorite color combinations in interior design? Are they the same as those you use in fashion?

In both fashion and interior decoration, I do not like colors in general . . . and I like "flashy" colors even less. Black, beige, and stone are the colors I use in my fashion designs and in my interior. Even though I offer a few colored pieces in my collections, the dresses that meet with the most success are those I like most, in golden beige hues, or pieces in beige shades with embroideries in similar colors. It is really the company's big success.

What are your favorite materials?

For me, every house should have some wood, some stone, and some fabric. But I like monochrome, and a certain unity in each room.

If you were an era, which would you be?
Ancient Rome, or the 1950s.

Do fabrics play an important part in your interior decoration? How do you use them?

Yes, of course, I believe beautiful textures to be very important . . . preferably thick, matte, solid materials whose feel I like.

In fashion, a cut of the scissors or a seam is of crucial importance. What aspects are most important in interior decoration?

If an interior design is very pure you can see everything, and consequently all the flaws as well. It is therefore essential to pay close attention to details: These must be perfectly studied so that nothing mars the place.

I am highly perfectionist at home: I like it when everything is in its place. Even an ashtray that isn't in the right place can upset me. I think my children, too, like to live in this atmosphere, and anyway they have their own rooms, which come closer to their lifestyles!

As a fashion designer, what you create differs according to the season. Does this encourage you to change the décor of your houses often?

No, I don't like changing the décor of my houses. If I feel I'd like to live in a different setting, I prefer not to touch anything and to do something different elsewhere. I don't like do-it-yourself in anything I do. That is why I have several houses! Since I have been working with my architect, Chakib Richani, we have succeeded in making some really different places that I like very much. The strength of our relationship rests on the fact that Chakib is able to transpose the exterior to the interior; he does not do interior decoration, but invites the outside in, creating continuity.

What sort of atmosphere do you like to create in a house?

An atmosphere that reflects who I am, and where there is life.

If you were an item of furniture, what would you be?

*A large bed, because we spend
half our lives in bed.*

If you were a color, what would you be?
Stone.

If you were a piece of music?
Oriental or classical music.

Which is your favorite room at home?

I don't have an exact place. I feel good wherever I happen to sit, but preferably in a room where there is a lot of light and vision is not limited. As I am a bit claustrophobic, I cannot live in a small, intimate place! I like rooms where plenty of light streams in, because this gives me a lot of energy.

What small everyday pleasures does your home give you?

I like to move around my house. And in the morning I go down to the living room to have my coffee, especially in summer when the sun is not yet high and I can feel it warming me up little by little. I like that sensation that the earth is moving.

Do you have a motto in interior decoration?

Space and light.

Is decorating a house the same as clothing a body?

No, because in my working life I am not only a fashion designer. I like every sphere to have its own world. I cannot design a house like I design a dress, and I cannot design a car in the same way as an interior. Otherwise, it would be less enjoyable. ■

Junko Shimada

Like her designs, in which the fascinating skins of pythons and crocodiles are reinvented each season, Junko Shimada—that most Parisian of Japanese women—lavishly creates a teeming, unusual animal world in her house. Furniture, objects, and paintings here sing a marvelous ode to wild beauty.

If you were a house, what would you be?

A very attractive, traditional Japanese house.

Where did you acquire your taste for interior decoration?

As a child I often spent time with my grandmother, who lived with us in a small town by the sea, near Tokyo. There is no doubt that her "art of living" influenced me a great deal. She loved looking after animals: She had cats, dogs, goldfish, and even chicks. She also knew how to look after the house shrewdly, using mere trifles: a simple flower placed delicately in a vase, for example. In the garden, there was a little house in which she wove silk, making her own dye from flowers that she picked and crushed in a mortar.

I still remember the day when we found that a huge snake had decided to make this silk house its home. I was horrified, but my grandmother reassured me, for this snake was, according to her, a sign of divine protection. Since then, I have surrounded myself with all these slightly "mythical" animals. . . . All this comes from my childhood. It is perhaps also the reason why, in my collections, I like to create garments of python skin which protect like a breastplate.

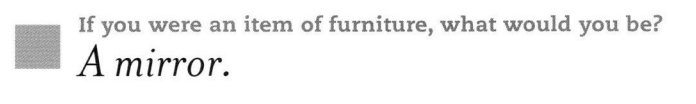

If you were an item of furniture, what would you be?

A mirror.

Are your sources of inspiration the same both for fashion and interior decoration?

Yes, probably, though it's hard for me to know exactly what they are. . . . The animal certainly represents, in all events, a link between my clothes and my interior decoration.

Are you interested in architecture? Who is your favorite architect?

Architecture fascinates me, and being an architect carries a great responsibility. . . . I like the work of the Mexican architect Luis Barragán a great deal; the colors he uses look magnificent under the Mexican sun. I also like Le Corbusier, especially his furniture.

What is your favorite decorative style?

In general, decoration bores me if it entails too much effort. The idea of hiring an interior designer to furnish my house would never cross my mind. However, I like certain designers such as Philippe Stark, who handles modernism with humor.

What are your favorite color combinations in interior design? Are they the same as those you use in fashion?

I find all fixed color combinations boring. I combine all colors, whether very bright or very dull: anthracite gray and midnight blue, with a very luminous pink, for example. My choice of colors is very spontaneous, above all.

What are your favorite materials?

I love the purity of crystal and the roughness of forged iron.

If you were a color, what would you be?
Midnight China blue.

Do fabrics play an important part in your interior decoration? How do you use them?

Clearly, in light of my childhood, I am very attracted to silk, all kinds of silk, whether they are very fine, like muslin or organza, or thicker, like taffeta. I am equally fond of linen and leather.

In fashion, a cut of the scissors or a seam is of crucial importance. What aspects are most important in interior decoration?

I don't have carefully studied details at home. I go with what takes my fancy. However, I like small details, such as the rainbows that a crystal prism diffuses over a wall, or the modern touch that white metal gives, for example.

If you were a fabric, what would you be?

A linen sheet.

If you were a piece of music, what would you be?

All music where the cello is heard.

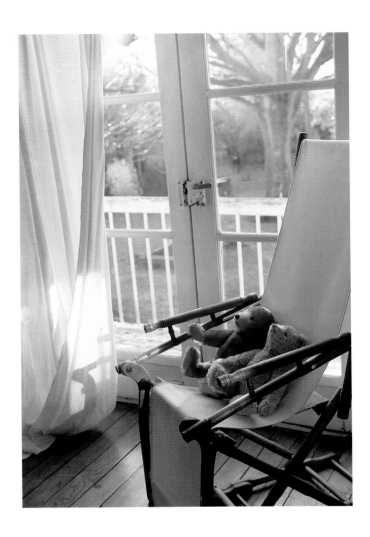

As a fashion designer, what you create differs according to the season. Does this encourage you to change the décor of your house often?

My tastes have remained the same for a long time. I add, remove, or move a piece of furniture from time to time—that's just about all.

What sort of atmosphere do you like to create in a house?

I like peace and well-being.

Which is your favorite room at home?

I spend most of my time in intimate, quiet rooms like my bedroom and the kitchen. The living room is too big for me.

What small everyday pleasures does your home give you?

When I have friends to visit, I like to spend a pleasant time with them here. But I do not suffer from loneliness when I am alone. I lie down in the living room–library next to my bedroom to read: bliss.

Do you have a motto in interior decoration?

None, only to do what seems right to you.

Is decorating a house the same as clothing a body?

The principle is the same, in fact. However, when you create a collection, you must be precise and coherent: You want to tell a story. It is not as spontaneous an act as decorating my house. ■

Giambattista Valli

When the Roman Giambattista Valli settled in Paris, his taste for eclecticism and love of travel fitted in spontaneously. Different eras blend together, and art mingles freely with craftsmanship in his "nomad's house," as he likes to call it.

If you were an item of furniture, what would you be?
*An armchair where one feels secure,
where one loves to read. Or a mirror.*

If you were an era, what would you be?
The 1960s and 1970s: According to friends who lived through those years, I would have loved them.

If you were a house?
A Japanese house, or an old abandoned palace.

Where did you acquire your taste for interior decoration?

My taste, in general terms, developed in Rome; I was born and raised in that city. That is where I learned to look at things. . . . In Rome there is a great mixture of styles, which coexist and create a fascinating rhythm: the style of ancient Rome, of the Renaissance, Baroque, Fascist, and contemporary architecture. I like eclecticism and I don't like the lukewarm. I am quite radical in my tastes.

Are you interested in architecture? Who is your favorite architect?

I always refer to my work. For me, architecture is like a well-cut dress: When a dress is very well cut it can be in any color or pattern and it will work. When space is well cut, as in the architecture of Frank Lloyd Wright, which I adore, anything can go in there . . . the cut is the foundation of everything.

Are your sources of inspiration the same both for fashion and interior decoration?

It's quite similar, because I don't try to do interior decoration. My houses have always been those of a nomad . . . where nothing is fixed.

My interior decoration is, more than anything else, evidence of what has aroused my passions in life. I fall in love with a fabric in India, I bring it home; I fall in love with a lamp, and I bring it home in my baggage. . . . It's the same with furniture, except that I like it to be practical. . . . I am not obsessed by perfection in a house. I like spontaneity. It's like with clothes: You have to leave some of the interpretation to the woman who wears the dress. Each has their own way of living with it.

What is your favorite decorative style?

At the moment, I want to surround myself with objects and fabrics that I am collecting. I don't like the idea of going to the flea market to hunt things. Instead of searching, I prefer to come upon things by chance, in a gallery or on a journey. . . . Then there is a story attached to them.

It's very odd because I love empty spaces. I remember that as a child in Rome, I attended a Catholic school—which is normal for a Roman!—and one day we went to visit St. Francis's house. In his bedroom, there was just a bed and a book! I said to myself that I would like to be able to attain that, one day. . . . People often talk about Japanese minimalism: It isn't just a matter of emptiness for emptiness's sake. It comes from a profound knowledge of different cultures and Western and Chinese decorative art, which the Japanese have gradually refined. An almost empty space containing a beautiful piece of design is not minimalism. It is necessary to have experienced many things to get to such purity . . . I'm not there yet.

What are your favorite color combinations in interior design? Are they the same as those you use in fashion?

In all my houses there have always been touches of red—all kinds of red. I like colors. In Paris, where I work, I am permanently surrounded by colors so, at home, here, I don't have too many. . . . Well, there are some, anyway. . . . In my collections, I also always incorporate some touches of red. It is a bit like a woman who does not put on makeup, but from time to time puts on some lipstick. All women, at least once in their lives, have worn lipstick.

What are your favorite materials?

I can't say which material. . . . I have no limits. I like all materials that give a sense of design, even if it's an old one. An eighteenth-century Venetian mirror, a Murano chandelier, or an African bracelet that can be used as a weapon—all this is design. I am attracted to things that tell me a story. I often think: Who was the person who looked at herself in the mirror? How was she dressed? . . . I like the idea of something that has a history. It is the same with people: I am always curious about their life experiences. To grow old is to grow ever more unique.

Do fabrics play an important part in your interior decoration? How do you use them?

I like curtains. In my living room, the windows are hung with old Chinese curtains with trees and birds all along them. And when you look into the garden, you have the impression that it is like a continuation of the curtains. Once these have been drawn, the light that passes through them is sublime: luxury! For me, luxury is very subtle things like that. . . . Apart from that, I possess collections of Chinese mandarins' clothes and Japanese, Moroccan, and Turkish fabrics that I sometimes use in my designs.

If you were a color, what would you be?
Pontormo red or imperial yellow.

In fashion, a cut of the scissors or a seam is of crucial importance. What aspects are most important in interior decoration?

I like to create a quality of light that makes people comfortable and beautiful. Light is very important. . . . It must caress, caress objects and allow you to discover things.

In fact, there are three essential elements in a house: the quality of light, the quality of the music, and the quality of the drink! All the rest comes afterward.

As a fashion designer, what you create differs according to the season. Does this encourage you to change the décor of your house often?

I don't change things very often, but there is always evolution: I remove an object and replace it with one or two others. . . . I hate fixed things. I also like moving paintings about and hanging new ones.

If you were a painting, what would you be?

A [Francis] Bacon or a [Diego] Velázquez.

What sort of atmosphere do you like to create in a house?

When people enter here, they should feel in slightly unfamiliar surroundings, almost on holiday. I also like this house because, with its garden, it is like being in the country; it's quiet, and one sleeps well here.

Which is your favorite room at home?

I feel happy when I'm in the living room. I settle down on the sofa. . . . Surrounded by books, incense, candles, music . . . not forgetting the champagne for friends who drop in. . . . I write, I read, and I draw in this room.

What small everyday pleasures does your home give you?

Simply (especially in spring and summer) to wake up in the morning, open the windows, and hear the birds singing; it's lovely. And I love walking on the parquet flooring, making it creak. I feel very comfortable here, even though some people think it's too intense.

Do you have a motto in interior decoration?

Never worry about lack of taste. I think anything can work. Also, when I enter a house, I do not seek to decorate it.

Is decorating a house the same as clothing a body?

When I clothe a body, I always think of the woman who is inside the garment. I dress her with my style, my taste, using my eye and my background. All this comes together, but it is done gently. Here, it's 100 percent me; my objects are part of my life, of the people I have met, of my travels. In my collections and in my house, there is this same blend of rigor and imagination. I try to find a balance in extremes. ■

If you were a fabric, what would you be?

All of them: It depends on my mood
on the day. But if I had to choose one,
it would be very high-quality cotton—
a white shirt, for example.

Diane Von Furstenberg

The draped, bosom-revealing dresses of Diane Von Furstenberg made her reputation in the 1970s. Even today her collections testify to her taste for a sophisticated femininity. In the same spirit, her spacious country house near New York, which looks airily over a lovely tree-filled park, underlines her natural elegance.

If you were a painting, what would you be?

A [Piet] Mondrian.

If you were an item of furniture, what would you be?
A big table.

Where did you acquire your taste for interior decoration?

I like my house. . . . This is where I find my peace, my strength, my rest. I have therefore designed my house like my life. I like space, big tables, books, luxurious comfort.

Are your sources of inspiration the same both for fashion and interior decoration?

Life inspires me: how to live, how to dress to be at ease and aesthetically pleasing.

Are you interested in architecture? Who is your favorite architect?

I would have loved to be an architect, and I love architecture. . . . Mies van der Rohe and [Luis] Barragán are among the architects whose simplicity and elegance I admire.

What is your favorite decorative style?

I like modernism and I like space. Modernism respects space and makes the most of it.

What are your favorite color combinations in interior design? Are they the same as those you use in fashion?

I like colors to be eclectic. I like the unexpected in life and in interior decoration . . . but I like it to be natural, and not forced.

What are your favorite materials?

I like wood, and big tables, because they can be used for everything.

Do fabrics play an important part in your interior decoration? How do you use them?

I adore all fabrics, especially ikats and brocades, among others. I collect the textiles that inspire me in my work.

In fashion, a cut of the scissors or a seam is of crucial importance. What aspects are most important in interior decoration?

Objects, furniture: Everything revolves around these.

If you were a house, what would you be?
My own house.

As a fashion designer, what you create differs according to the season. Does this encourage you to change the décor of your house often?
The interior lives and develops as life goes on.

What sort of atmosphere do you like to create in a house?
Luxury, through a high level of comfort, as well as very beautiful objects and furniture.

Which is your favorite room at home?
I love my studio. It is the place where I sleep and work. I could stay there for months on end.

If you were a fabric, what would you be?
Silk.

Biographies

Manish Arora was intrigued by fashion as a means of self-expression at a rather young age; he studied at the National Institute of Fashion Technology in New Delhi, India, graduating in 1995, then launched his eponymous brand in 1997.

■ In 1998, he presented his first collection at the Park Hotel in New Delhi. The press was enthusiastic, seeing in him a rising star of Indian fashion. His designs were immediately sold in prestigious shops, such as Carma in New Delhi, Folio in Bangalore, and Kali in Calcutta. He presented his second collection in New Delhi in 1999.

He launched a second line, Fish Fry, in 2000, presenting his collection, in association with Bacardi, in six Indian cities. His designs began to be seen at Lord & Taylor in New York. He took part in a spectacular fashion parade on the theme of "kitsch," held at the India Habitat Center in New Delhi.

In 2002, he opened his first shop in New Delhi and took part in an art installation at Selfridges in London. During the New Delhi fashion week, he presented his collection, and many shops in Indian cities began to stock his label.

In 2003, he opened his second shop in Mumbai, where his collection met with great success during the city's fashion week. The Parisian shop Maria Luisa also fell for his designs, and Arora began to export to eight shops in Europe.

In 2004, he took part in his fifth fashion week in India. He received the award for best women's ready-to-wear designer, the first-ever fashion prize given in Mumbai.

■ In May 2005, during Miami's fashion week, his collection was named best collection of the year. He received the award for best designer at the 2005 MTV Lycra Style Awards in Mumbai.

■ Manish Arora presented his collection in London for the first time during that city's 2005 fall fashion week, where he was received with enthusiasm by the press and buyers alike. He set up his company in England in association with the Center for Fashion Enterprise, and in December of the same year, he opened a shop in Lodhi Colony Market, New Delhi. Some of his designs were exhibited at the Global Local exhibition at the Victoria & Albert Museum, London.

■ In February 2006, during his fashion show in London, the most distinguished journalists were unanimous in their praise. His collections were now on sale in nearly seventy-five shops around the world.

As well as featuring in many articles in a number of magazines worldwide, he made the cover of the prestigious Indian magazine *Outlook,* which pronounced him to be the best Indian designer.

■ A Manish Arora franchise was opened in Kuwait in September 2006. Levi's has suggested that he lend his signature to a collection for the international market.

■ Manish Arora says he wants to be free to create, without being influenced by any trends. His sources of inspiration are many, but he is very attached to Oriental culture, Bollywood films, and Indian music. He loves to combine bright colors and intricate detail with urban styles where humor is always present, to render women at once intimidating, sporty, and joyous.

Damiano Biella was born in Milan, Italy, on November 21, 1970. Ever since the age of six, when he attended a show by Valentino, he has loved fashion. He was instantly bewitched by the femininity and sumptuous appearance of the collection being shown, and from that time onward began to create designs.

■ In 1984, he entered the Milan Art Institute, leaving in 1989 with his diploma in art, design, and graphic art. At the time, he saw design as an alternative to art, and it endowed him with a broader general education. Armed with his diploma, he worked for design and graphic art companies, but his true passion was still fashion.

He began his fashion career in 1991 with Gucci, in Florence, as an assistant stylist. Two years later, he became the women's ready-to-wear stylist at Céline in Paris, where he stayed until 1998.

■ That year he left for New York, where he was employed as artistic director of the Carolina Herrera Company. Responsible for ready-to-wear, furs, and wedding gowns, he was also in charge of fashion parades and communications.

In collaboration with the shoe specialist Manolo Blahnik, he designed a collection of accessories for the brand.

■ Biella joined the Valentino fashion house, based in Rome, in 2003 as director of collections. He worked closely with Valentino Garavani on all collections, including Valentino Couture. Responsible for different lines, such as ready-to-wear, Valentino Roma, and Valentino Uomo, as well as licensing, he was also put in charge of the creative side of fashion shows and communications.

Biella had always been an admirer of Valentino's highly feminine creations. He valued Valentino's skill, constant quest for beautiful colors, and attention to detail in a lavish aesthetic approach devoted to women.

■ In 2006, the Escada Company in Germany called on his talent and offered him the post of artistic director. He was then in charge of the brand's global identity, as well as all the Escada and Escada Sport collections. He also took care of the development of the accessory collections and licenses, especially the perfumes.

He produced his first Escada collection for autumn/winter 2007–2008, working with a team of twenty stylists.

■ Damiano Biella has remained faithful to the style he has adored since childhood: highly feminine lines, with a contemporary classic quality and timeless luxury. He likes to create for women who are popular with men.

Born on July 21, 1967, Vanessa Bruno had a predisposition for the world of fashion, as her Danish mother and Italian father both worked in this sphere. She started in the business as an adolescent, aged 15, working as a model for Dorothée Bis and as a trainee at Cacharel. Her first early steps in the profession made it clear to her that her true place was not on the catwalk but in the design studio.

A one-year stay in Montreal triggered the changeover, and she had found her vocation. "There," she says, "there was no designer; we bought our clothes in the flea market. That was how I discovered old-style men's materials (herringbone, flannel), and I decided to try to adapt them for women's designs." This aim was to guide her future decisions.

■ Bruno joined Daniel Hechter in 1989 as the head of the women's collection.

She opened a first outlet in the Marais district of Paris, where she offered a minicollection inspired by the most varied forms: A personal style began to take shape.

■ In 1996, she launched her brand and rapidly made her mark. A second line, "Athé," appeared in 1997. Passionate about her job and very determined, in 1998 she opened, thanks to a Japanese partner who met her standards, her first shop in the heart of the Saint-Germain-des-Prés district in Paris, followed by seven outlets in Japan—especially in Tokyo, where she became a veritable star.

The same year, Bruno created a line of accessories that included her famous spangled basket, which became a phenomenal success. Her designs were now sold not only in her shops in Saint-Germain-des-Prés and on the right bank of the Seine in Paris, but also in the prestigious department stores Bon Marché and Printemps.

In 2004, she launched the Vanessa Bruno lingerie line, and the following year her eponymous jeans line.

In November 2005, she opened a new shop in a district for which she had a particular affection—the Marais.

Bruno likes to draw inspiration from what is around her: music, design, cinema . . . and women.

She has clothed not only actresses seduced by her simple designs and her feeling for textiles, but an entire generation of active, feminine women. She likes to create "easy garments for difficult women."

■ This singular young designer presents her collection each season through an installation that combines several artistic influences, including photography, film, drawing, and musical performance. In this way, her creative landscape and engaging personality are revealed.

Patrick Cox was born in Canada and spent part of his childhood in Chad. Since his earliest childhood he has had a veritable passion for British culture, admiring the punk scene and the Queen in equal measure. He decided to turn his dreams into reality and, in 1983, went to study shoe styling at Cordwainers Technical College, London. On leaving college, he began to design shoes for fashion designers such as Vivienne Westwood and John Galliano.

■ He launched his own collection in September 1985, meeting with immediate success within a circle of cognoscenti who dubbed him the "shoe guru." In 1991, he opened his first shop in Symmons Street.

In 1993, he designed a new line of shoes, called "Wannabe." When the collection was launched, a crowd of fans besieged his shop, eager to have the privilege of being among the first to buy one or more pairs from the collection.

Orders flowed in, leading Cox to open more shops, including his first in Paris, France, in July 1994.

At the end of his label's first decade, Cox won the Accessory Stylist of the Year prize awarded by the British Fashion Council. International recognition brought him other prestigious prizes.

From then on, the brand became extraordinarily famous. Cox was admired for his creativity and the ingenuity of his style. His talent led him to be appointed artistic director of the celebrated Charles Jourdan brand, where he was put in charge of overhauling the collections to give them a younger look. After two years working for this label, he decided to concentrate on developing his own business.

Twenty years after he started out in the world of fashion, Patrick Cox remains unquestionably at the forefront, always in search of the new shapes, new inspiration, and new details that have largely contributed to his fame. The fact that some of his designs have been put on show in museums, as well as his commercial success, have assured him a long-standing presence in his field.

His shoes are worn by celebrities including Elizabeth Hurley, Lenny Kravitz, Elton John, and Gwen Stefani, among others, who find in his collections the originality and flamboyance they crave. Cox sells his collections in England, France, Hong Kong, and Japan.

■ Deeply involved in human rights, the designer was appointed president of the creative committee of Amnesty International, for which he was put in charge of helping internal teams in devising new publicity and fundraising campaigns.

■ To mark the sixtieth anniversary of the famous Fender guitar brand, Cox—a lifelong lover of music—customized a guitar with python skin, calling it "Snakebite." Sixty custom models were produced for the "Rock Couture" exhibition by various big names of music, fashion, and design, and shown at the Galeries Lafayette in Paris and the Harrods Rock event in London.

■ As passionately interested as he was on his first day, Patrick Cox carries out his work with a characteristic sense of humor, incorporating details into his designs that are always original and a touch eccentric, combined with impeccable quality of finish—which makes him one of the world's most talented shoe designers.

#50-65 Dolce & Gabbana

Domenico Dolce was born in Polizzi Generosa, in the province of Palermo, on August 13, 1958. He started work very young, in his father's tailoring business.

Stefano Gabbana was born in Milan on November 14, 1962. After studying graphic design, he worked for various advertising agencies.

■ The two designers met in the early 1980s in the design studio where they were both working as assistants. After several joint projects, they opened their own design studio under the name Dolce & Gabbana. In October 1985 they presented their first women's collection as part of the "new talents collections" show held in Milan.

■ Over time, the two designers' profound Italian roots and the elegance, poetry, and humor displayed by their creations caught the attention of the international press and of the most discriminating buyers, and so, season after season, with creativity, determination, and passion, Dolce & Gabbana became pivotal figures in Italian fashion. For their advertising campaigns, they used some of the most celebrated photographers and models, bringing an enthusiastic reaction from the press and from buyers, and their clothes were made in collaboration with the clothing business founded by Domenico Dolce's family at Legnano.

■ In April 1989, Dolce & Gabbana presented their women's collection in Tokyo for the first time. They launched their first men's collection in 1990. In April of that year, they organized their first men's and women's show in New York. They produced their first perfume, Dolce & Gabbana Parfum, in 1992; it was awarded the international best women's perfume prize by the Accademia del Profumo in 1993.

■ Dolce & Gabbana's showrooms grew in number, and new horizons opened up for them. In 1993 they were asked by the pop singer Madonna to create fifteen hundred costumes for her Girlie Show tour. This international recognition marked the start of a close relationship between the designers and the worlds of music and cinema. They designed stage costumes for Whitney Houston, Kylie Minogue, Mary J. Blige, and many others.

■ In 1994, a new, younger Dolce & Gabbana line appeared. In the space of a few years, it became phenomenally successful. In 2001, the D&G Junior line debuted.

Dolce & Gabbana pour Homme was introduced in 1994. In 1995, it won the international Accademia del Profumo prize for best men's scent, best packaging, and best ad campaign. In 1996 it won the French "Oscar des Parfums," a first for an Italian scent. In 1997, they created By Dolce & Gabbana, a unisex perfume, which was followed in 1999 by D&G Masculine and D&G Feminine. In 2001, a new women's perfume, Dolce & Gabbana Light Blue, was born, followed in 2003 by Sicily Dolce & Gabbana.

From 1999 onward, Dolce & Gabbana added glasses, underwear, swimwear, scarves, and ties to their line. They acquired new factories and opened several new shops under their own name all over the world. With the passing seasons they collected many prizes for their work, their collections, and their advertising campaigns, and the designers were commissioned to create the official kit for the Italian team at the 2006 World Cup in Germany.

■ The Dolce & Gabbana story has been marked by constant development but has also remained faithful to the original ideal of these two designers: a passion for a sensual, Mediterranean type of fashion, filled with both wit and glamour, and simultaneously innovative, creative, and luxurious.

#66-75 Jacopo Etro

Today, the Etro label unites its poetic, colorful vision through its collections, comprising women's and men's ready-to-wear, accessories, household furnishings, and perfumes. Gimmo Etro founded his fabrics business in Milan, Italy, in 1968. Today, he shares the running of the company with his children: Jacopo, Kean, Ippolito, and Veronica.

■ The Etro fashion house is famous for its luxurious fabrics with highly distinctive prints and patterns.

It was one of the first fabric brands to have looked to the countries of the East for its sources of inspiration, and the only one to integrate an overall cultural and artistic concept for each of its lines.

■ Each of Gimmo Etro's children runs a division of the brand. Jacopo, the eldest, inherited his father's passion for textiles and began learning under him at a very early age. Born in Milan in 1962, he studied economics and politics in England. Nevertheless, his attachment to the family business brought him back to Milan, where he took charge of fashion accessories and household furnishings. He also designs the fabric collections for both fashion and interior decoration.

Kean is the stylist for the men's collections, Ippolito is the finance director, and Veronica designs the women's collections. Each contributes his or her own vision to the label's style with passion and creativity acquired at the heart of the business.

■ Strengthened by its success, the Etro house has naturally diversified.

In 1981, the family business began to manufacture fabrics for furnishing. In 1983, the brand developed accessory lines comprising scarves, ties, and shawls. In 1984, the business launched its lines of handbags and luggage.

That year also saw an expansion of retail activity.

Since 1985, Etro has included among its products a line of perfumes, as well as men's and women's ready-to-wear, shoe collections, and lines of eyewear.

Shops have been opened in Milan, Rome, Florence, Bologna, Verona, and Venice.

Over time, Etro has also opened shops in Paris, New York, London, Tokyo, Madrid, Berlin, and Moscow, among other places.

Etro collections are also sold in more than 300 department stores worldwide.

There is unquestionably a connecting thread running back to the label's beginnings, from cashmere prints to collections and shops. Each design is conceived and intended as an authentic piece of art, singular and elegant.

Loulou de la Falaise was born in England, into a large aristocratic and artistic family; her Irish mother, Maxime, was Schiaparelli's favorite model, and her father was Count Alain de la Falaise. Loulou attended an English boarding school, taking full advantage of her adolescence spent in London. In her youth she allowed free rein to her imagination, which was to fuel her future creations. At first she worked as fashion editor on *Harper's Bazaar*. It was there in New York, where she had followed her mother in the 1960s, that Loulou entered the world of fashion, promising a fine career. A friend of Robert Mapplethorpe and Andy Warhol, she became a model for *Vogue* and was photographed by the most prestigious photographers, including Helmut Newton, while also designing prints for Halston.

■ In 1968, she had a chance encounter with Yves Saint Laurent. The couturier, captivated by Loulou's singular attitude, asked her to join his team, which she did in 1972.

Loulou was to bring to the Saint Laurent label all the qualities the designer had perceived, as well as an exceptional taste in colors and an imagination that enabled her, as her mother used to say, to "dress someone with nothing but some old clothes and a safety pin." She was to exercise her talent in designing some two thousand pieces of jewelry for Yves Saint Laurent's various collections.

The friendship between the two designers became so strong that Yves Saint Laurent, aided by Pierre Bergé, organized the young woman's marriage to Thadée Klossowski de Rola, son of the painter Balthus, in 1977.

■ When, after thirty years of working together, Yves Saint Laurent retired, Loulou realized her dream, opening an English fashion house in Paris in 2003. In the Rue de Bourgogne, her brother Alexis—an architect specializing in interiors—designed a place rich in colors and precious materials, reflecting his sister's passion for flowers and exotic destinations. This flagship store offered a line of very brightly colored jewelry and unimaginable materials, created by Loulou with her unparalleled sense of color and detail. Her popularity grew very quickly, and her label acquired an international profile, from Tokyo to New York, from Casablanca to Hong Kong, and in the capitals of Europe.

Flush with these successes, Loulou opened a shop on the Right Bank of the Seine, in Rue Cambon. Here, as in all her other ventures, the designer energetically conveys all the magic of her brightly colored collections of jewelry, accessories, and knitwear.

Martin Grant was born on August 2, 1966, in Melbourne, Australia. It was there that he launched his first ready-to-wear line in 1982 and opened his first workshop-showroom in the trendy artists' district of Little Collins Street. He became popular with fashion magazines and professionals, and in 1988, he won the prestigious Cointreau Young Designer Award in Sydney. At the age of twenty-one, success was within his grasp, but he felt a need to explore other techniques: Moving away from the world of fashion, he studied sculpture at the Victorian College of Arts. Four years later, he missed working with bodies and materials; he left for London, where he perfected his technique in bespoke tailoring under Koji Tatsuno.

■ In 1992, Grant settled in Paris, France. He presented his first collections at the Hôpital Éphémère in Montmartre—small selections of twenty or so pieces that enabled him gradually to build up a loyal following of customers and to sell in Japan, Australia, and England.

In 1996, he opened his shop in a former barber shop in the Marais district of Paris. In August 2005, Grant's workshop and store moved into an apartment, an ideal, refined space where his customers could choose from his whole current collection and also see that of the previous season. With time, Grant found himself presenting his collections to an audience of connoisseurs with a preference for events with an intimate feel.

■ Offering timeless silhouettes with pure lines, his style is marked by an almost sculptural charm and elegance, with carefully researched details. A military quality gives functionality to these structured forms, refined but always feminine. The body is emphasized and enhanced.

Thanks to the cut of his coats and jackets, simultaneously simple and spectacular, and impeccably finished, Martin Grant enthralled an international high-end market, notably the likes of Barneys and Neiman Marcus, as well as private clients such as Cate Blanchett. His designs have been sold in Paris, New York, Chicago, Los Angeles, Seattle, Boston, London, Milan, Brescia, Moscow, Berlin, Munich, Vienna, Dubai, Hong Kong, Taipei, Tokyo, Yokohama, Osaka, Fukuoka, Sydney, Auckland, Toronto, and Athens.

■ Since September 2003, he has been responsible for styling the collections of Barneys Private Label.

■ Along with his work in fashion, Grant has taken part for several years in various artistic projects, emphasizing the link he makes between design and sculpture, including crinolines on the statues of the château at Courances (1994); the "100 Headless Women" exhibition in Australia and at Selfridges in London (1997); a luminous crinoline skirt for the Absolut 2000 calendar (1999); and the "Autour du Miroir" ("Around the Mirror") exhibition at the château at Courances (2004).

■ From December 8, 2005 to May 7, 2006, the National Gallery of Victoria in his hometown of Melbourne, Australia, held a retrospective exhibition, comprising clothes, drawings, photographs, sculpture, and film.

Betsey Johnson was born in 1942 in Connecticut. She got her Bachelors degree at Syracuse University. The determining factor came into play during her childhood, for her dearest wish was to become a dancer. She devoted much energy to this—a foretaste of her later dynamism—but at the same time she took a great interest in the costumes. It was in these two spheres that she would find her sources of inspiration, and the creativity of her collections would bear the marks of this. Her theatrical entry, parading about on the catwalk during the final bow at each of her fashion parades, would also contribute to her reputation.

■ A prizewinner at the competition run by *Mademoiselle* magazine in 1964 for a "guest editor," she entered the world of New York fashion. Starting the following year her designs were sold, together with those of other young designers, in a fashionable shop. Her style, featuring an impeccable cut but at the same time sexy and with a hippie quality, immediately became established.

■ Johnson married the guitarist of the rock group Velvet Underground, and became part of the fashionable New York scene. Her husband, John Cale, wore her designs on stage and in town. In 1969, divorced, the young designer opened a shop—Betsey Bunki Nini—and accepted an invitation from Alvin Dunskin to go and work in San Francisco. For several years, she divided her time between the East and West Coasts of the United States, while new opportunities presented themselves, including a proposal from the Alley Cat brand, standard-bearer of the bohemian and ethnic dress styles of rock 'n' roll.

■ In 1972 she won the prestigious Coty, the youngest designer ever to receive the award.

■ Johnson's great professional leap came in 1978, when she set up, together with her associate Chantal Bacon, a label in her own name, and was thus able to allow her personal view of fashion a free rein. The unfailingly impeccable cut of her garments, the floral prints of her dresses, and her taste for imaginative details clearly revealed her style.

■ From then on, shops were opened one after the other: in the heart of Soho, New York, on Melrose Avenue in Los Angeles, then in London in 1998, opening the floodgates to international expansion—Vancouver, Toronto, and, in 2006, the first shop in Tokyo.
   Moreover, Johnson sells her collections in more than a thousand department stores across the United States, Europe, and Asia. Indefatigable, she lends her signature to licenses for shoes and lingerie, and includes in her collections bags, belts, watches, jewelry, and even a perfume. Thus she offers, thanks to her diversification, a veritable art of living. It is not surprising that, over the years, she has regularly received recognition for her contribution to American fashion!

■ Her engaging personality, her strength of character, her courage in the face of illness, and her generous and active involvement in the fight against cancer have made Johnson an exemplar for many women. With her unflagging enthusiasm, she carries out her work always with the same passion, and her unique style transcends the generations.

■ The generosity of this artist comes across clearly in her profession of faith: "Making clothes involves what I like . . . color, pattern, shape and movement. . . . I like the everyday process . . . the people, the pressure, the surprise of seeing the work come alive walking and dancing around on strangers." On this evidence, Betsey Johnson's life must look very rosy.

José Lévy was born in Paris, France, in 1963. He was attracted to artistic design, and this led him to enroll at the ESMOD school of design in Paris. On completing his studies there in 1983, he won first prize with his men's collection.

■ He began his career as a stylist by working freelance for various international companies and style studios, including Le Printemps Brummel, Woolmark International, Les 3 Suisses, and the Peclers and Nelly Rodi agencies.

■ In 1990, he presented his personal collection at the SEHM male ready-to-wear fashion show, where he won the first prize. As the seasons went by, his mischievous style, marked by childlike details, such as small bands of color and schoolboy checks, became purer and simpler, without losing its eccentric side. Playing with conventions, he reinvented the male wardrobe with originality, elegance, and a palette of colors where blues, from the softest to the most intense, are often in the limelight.

■ Lévy joined the Cacharel label as artistic director for the men's line, and in 1994 collaborated with the Nina Ricci Monsieur fashion house as an image and product consultant.
   In 1996, he was awarded the prestigious Grand Prix de la Ville de Paris (an artistic prize given by the city of Paris) for best designer of the year.
   Aside from this work, he designed the Something By collections for the Japanese group Edwin, while consulting for big retail brands such as Monoprix and Rodier Homme.

■ From 1998 onward, he was artistic director of the British luxury brand Holland & Holland, responsible for its market positioning, visual identity, fashion shows, and advertising. Lévy imbued this brand, something of an institution, with his assertive, poetic style.

■ In 1999, he opened his first shop, in the Marais district of Paris, and in 2001 the department stores Le Bon Marché and Galeries Lafayette opened spaces for the José Lévy collections.

■ He discontinued his label in 2003 and became a consultant for Dim. At the same time, he designed a limited edition collection of men's and women's shoes and bags for André. In 2004, Lévy was appointed artistic director for the Emanuel Ungaro men's line. He defined the parameters of a modern elegance in keeping with the ultrafeminine Emanuel Ungaro women's collections. He did not hesitate to use the tiger skin motif, recast in black and white, or prints of tropical flowers in shades of fuchsia and ultraviolet.

■ Strange and eclectic, Lévy touches on various creative spheres, going from fashion to photography, music, and design. The composer Benjamin Biolay wrote music exclusively for his autumn/winter fashion show in 2003, and Lévy's own interest in design led him to lend his signature to a line of porcelain for the Deshoulières group. He turned his hand with equal facility to designing furniture, mirrors, and lighting for Éditions Corinne.
   His tastes regularly lead him to embark on fruitful joint artistic projects. Notably, he has worked with the photographer Jack Pierson and taken part with the architect Xavier Gonzales in "Arch-Couture," an original exhibition that presents the collaborative work of several creative pairings. He has designed carpets for Aubusson for an exhibition that also featured Sonia Rykiel, Jean-Paul Gaultier, Jean-Charles de Castelbajac, and Emanuel Ungaro.

■ José Lévy's protean talent is striking, and it is the reason his world is so seductive. It augurs well for his future creations.

#116-125 Christian Louboutin

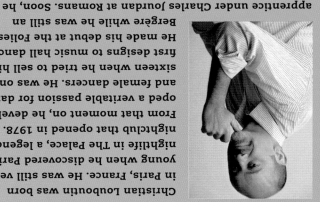

Christian Louboutin was born in Paris, France. He was still very young when he discovered Parisian nightlife in The Palace, a legendary nightclub that opened in 1978. From that moment on, he developed a veritable passion for dance and female dancers. He was only sixteen when he tried to sell his first designs to music hall dancers. He made his debut at the Folies Bergère while he was still an apprentice under Charles Jourdan at Romans. Soon, he was working freelance for such Italian and French fashion houses as Maud Frison, Chanel, Yves Saint Laurent, and Sidonie Larizzi. In 1988, he teamed up with Roger Vivier, the legendary shoe designer and associate of Christian Dior. While preparing a retrospective on Vivier's work, he discovered shoes created for the coronation of the Shah of Iran and a pair of diamond pumps made for Marlene Dietrich.

■ In 1992, he opened his first shop in Paris: The Christian Louboutin fashion house was born. His first designs (such as Love and Trash) presented extremely feminine garments. Combining glamour with wit, they won immediate praise from the press and discerning customers. He also brought an Italian flair that ensured that his designs had an incomparable finish. Inspired by a love of gardens, a passion for the East, and many travels, which took him as far as Uzbekistan and Jordan, he decided to have a château built in Luxor, Egypt, on the left bank of the Nile.

■ From the outset, Louboutin's designs embodied a perfect blend of beauty and sex appeal for celebrities and elegant women the world over. His delicate shoes—easily recognized by their lacquered red soles—can be seen on the feet of the most beautiful actresses, including Nicole Kidman, Catherine Deneuve, Cameron Diaz, Gwyneth Paltrow, Kirsten Dunst, and Angelina Jolie, as well as singers Gwen Stefani, Destiny's Child, Tina Turner, Janet Jackson, and many members of royal families.

■ Louboutin also collaborates with famous fashion designers, such as Chloé, Lanvin, Roland Mouret, Diane von Furstenberg, Alexander McQueen, and Viktor & Rolf, and for some years he has supplied the shoes that accompany the creations of Jean-Paul Gaultier. Yves Saint Laurent associated his own name with that of another designer for the first time with the "Christian Louboutin for Yves Saint Laurent Haute Couture 1962-2002" line.

■ With the same creative verve, Louboutin launched a line of handbags, which echoed his shoe collection.

■ Louboutin's designs are sold in the most prestigious department stores and shops in Los Angeles, New York, Moscow, and Hong Kong, as well as in Paris, where he has his two flagship stores. Each shop, designed and decorated by the designer himself, reflects the spirit of his fashion house. Although they are different, and decorated with furniture from all over the world, they convey that *je ne sais quoi* that embodies the brand's aesthetic: the elegance of Parisian style and unreserved devotion to women.

#126-131 Catherine Malandrino

Born in Grenoble, France, Catherine Malandrino attended the ESMOD school of design, where she studied styling. After gaining her diploma, she started her career in Paris, working for the Dorothée Bis, Louis Féraud, and Emanuel Ungaro brands.

■ For five years during the 1990s, she was style director for the Et Vous brand. Malandrino moved to New York in 1998 after meeting her husband and future associate Bernard Aidan. There, she relaunched Diane Von Furstenberg's collections.

That same year, she launched her own eponymous label and presented her first collection, "Collage." Her designs immediately conveyed her style, which was light and feminine but at the same time rigorous in the cut of the garments. She asserted that she wanted to "bring gentleness and refinement to a feminine, urban wardrobe, and to help women show their individuality and personality through their clothes."

In 2000, she reproduced the American flag on garments including muslin dresses and T-shirts in her collection entitled "Flag." This collection, acclaimed by the press, was an immediate hit with the public and with celebrities such as Madonna, who wore her T-shirt on stage during her world tour. The muslin dress from this iconic line became part of the Zandra Rhodes collection in the Fashion and Textile Museum in London.

In 2001, Catherine Malandrino presented her "Hallelujah" fashion show at the renowned Apollo Theater. At the same time, she designed a special collection for the singer Mary J. Blige.

In 2002 came further confirmation of her status in the eyes of all fashion fans when the cult series *Sex and the City* used as a setting Catherine Malandrino's first shop in the Soho district. She then designed a collection for the highly popular star Sarah Jessica Parker.

On the back of this success, the designer launched, in 2002, a second, more luxurious and exclusive line, comprising ninety pieces produced in limited numbers, and a dress for Demi Moore.

2004 saw the opening of her flagship boutique in Manhattan's Meat-Packing District; the shop's interior was designed in collaboration with the designer Christophe Pillet.

In a move aimed at reconnecting with her French roots, Catherine Malandrino opened her first Paris shop, in the Saint-Germain-des-Prés district. The same year, she launched her shoe and bag collections. In association with Repetto, the brand specializing in dance clothing and accessories, she designed a ballerina shoe that took up the "Star-Spangled Banner" motif from her "Flag" collection.

■ Malandrino's designs, which combine unconventionality with contrast and femininity, have met with unquestionable success in many countries—including Japan, France, America, and China—where they have been distributed.

■ From the beginning, Catherine Malandrino has always conveyed through her designs a sensuality and dynamism appropriate to a woman who likes to "design irresistible clothes that make women desirable, clothes that a man would like to remove delicately."

Marcel Marongiu was born in Paris, France, in 1963 to a Swedish mother and a French-Italian father. He spent the first twenty years of his life in Stockholm, Sweden. He was attracted to painting at a very early age, drawing cartoon strips when he was four years old and dreaming of becoming a painter. Later, he began to paint, but this form of escapism was not to his family's taste. He therefore studied economics for three years, with little commitment, before finally attending a trade school and then going on to the Stockholm fine arts college. It was then that Marcel Marongiu realized that clothing could be his chosen medium.

■ In 1988, back in Paris, Marcel Marongiu set up the company that bears his name. From his very first women's collection, he showed an attraction for contrasting combinations: masculine and feminine, romanticism and sensuality, the structured and the deconstructed—all marked by his Scandinavian and Italian influences. His passion for painting also came through in each of his collections.

■ He opened his first shop in Paris's 6th arrondissement in 1994, followed by the second, in the Rue Saint-Honoré, in 1997, at the same time launching his leather goods line with clean, no-nonsense lines.

Marongiu's collections were also sold in large department stores such as the Galeries Lafayette and Le Bon Marché in Paris, as well as in the prestigious Isetan and Seibu shops in Japan and Nordstrom and Bergdorf Goodman in the United States.

■ In 2000, on the tenth anniversary of the founding of his company, he presented the "Composite" exhibition at Silvera in Paris, and later at the design museum in Stockholm.

That same year saw the launch of a line of porcelain tableware with pure, sensual lines, designed for Artoria.

Two years later, he created his men's collection, aimed at a the elegant man with "a minimum of self-knowledge and an indifference to fashion."

■ He held the exhibition "Hommes sous influence" ("Men Under the Influence") at the Musée des Beaux-Arts in Caen in 2003. This comprised an installation containing the main pieces from his collections, together with his various sources of inspiration in the areas of painting, cinema, music, and fashion.

■ He closed down his company in 2006 following disagreements with his Japanese partners. Thereafter he worked chiefly as artistic director for various labels in China and Japan, while also working on the interior decoration for several hotels in Sweden.

Marcel Marongiu's working life has been rich in a wide range of creative activities, and throughout he has always strived to fight against stereotypes.

Born in Paris, France, Gilles Mendel began his career in fashion very young. During his childhood, he began an apprenticeship under his father at the celebrated furrier J. Mendel. The history of this house began in 1870 when Joseph Breitman, furrier to the Russian nobility, founded the family business and laid down its guiding principle: exceptional quality both in the cut and in the materials used. Since then, the house of J. Mendel has remained faithful to this precept. At the end of World War II, the house of J. Mendel opened its shop in the Rue Saint-Honoré, Paris.

■ In 1982, Gilles Mendel moved to New York and opened a shop on Fifth Avenue, in the salon of Elizabeth Arden.

In 1985, he opened the first shop of his own, on Madison Avenue. This prestigious address remains, to this day, the brand's flagship store in the United States. Six more shops have been opened since then, in Aspen, Chicago, Hong Kong, Istanbul, New York, and Paris.

■ Once established in New York, Gilles Mendel became the darling of Manhattan's chic and elite. Thanks to his growing fame, constant requests for private fittings and special orders flooded in. These demands led him to make new designs and, by extension, to launch a complete luxury ready-to-wear collection.

■ In the space of four years, Mendel broadened his creative vision and diversified his work, producing six ready-to-wear collections with the same skill that brought him his renown as a furrier.

In recognition of his success, he was made a member of the CFDA (Council of Fashion Designers of America) in 2003, and now presents his fashion shows during fashion week under the tents of Bryant Park.

■ Mendel is unique for his use of exceptionally high quality materials, but also for his modern sense of style. He is bold enough to use fur on materials such as silk to produce designs for summer wear.

His daywear and evening dress collections quickly achieved notable critical and commercial success. The purity and clean quality of their lines is only an appearance, for the clothes are put together in a highly sophisticated way. For example, silk muslin and satin are cut, as the designer puts it, "to create different styles of volume and texture." Similarly, tweeds are put together and sewn by hand in order to enhance the body in a graceful way: delicate work that "comes from the heart." This quality of manufacture and the use of luxury materials in unexpected ways constitute Mendel's signature.

■ Not only has Gilles Mendel, through his designs, taken fur fashion forward, but also in his ready-to-wear collections he has shown the same care in the manufacture of his garments.

All of Mendel's creations attract a large clientele, including many Hollywood celebrities who share his taste for timeless, glamorous, refined fashion.

#152–163
Rick Owens

Rick Owens was born in 1962, and spent all his childhood in southern California. He began by studying art at the Parsons School of Design in Los Angeles before finally switching to a dressmaking course.

■ After working for several years for local textile companies, Owens set up his own company in 1994. His reputation and skill led him to meet a group of Italian manufacturers, with whom he teamed up.

In 2002, shortly after presenting his first collection in New York, he was awarded the Perry Ellis Emerging Talent Award by the CFDA (Council of Fashion Designers of America).

He describes his collections, often regarded as "gothic" by the press, as glamour meets grunge—on the basis of which he coined the term "glunge." Owens likes to make asymmetrical, deconstructed designs, which he combines with waist-hugging jackets, impeccably cut, in a palette of mineral colors, especially every possible shade of gray.

He has compared his style to a sculpture by Brancusi: "[Just] a slab of metal on a hunk of wood, but it's about the right piece of metal, the right hunk of wood, and the perfect gesture."

Having become the favorite stylist of rock stars and other clients who liked to cultivate an "avant-garde" look, Owens made the big leap and moved to Paris in 2003.

At the same time, the celebrated French furrier Révillon—founded in 1723—entrusted him with the artistic direction of its brand.

■ Owens was fascinated by design, and in 2005 launched his collection of furniture, inspired by the shapes of the designs of Eileen Grey and Brancusi, but also by Californian skate parks. He used original materials such as resin, fiberglass, cashmere, and bone to produce grandiose, extremely comfortable furniture.

■ He opened his shop in Paris in 2006, under the arcades of the Palais-Royal Garden. There he offers collections under his own label, those he designs for Révillon, and also some pieces of his own furniture.

■ Rick Owens likes to say that his garments are his autobiography: "They embody both the calm elegance I aspire to and the damage that is caused along the way."

#164–173
John Rocha

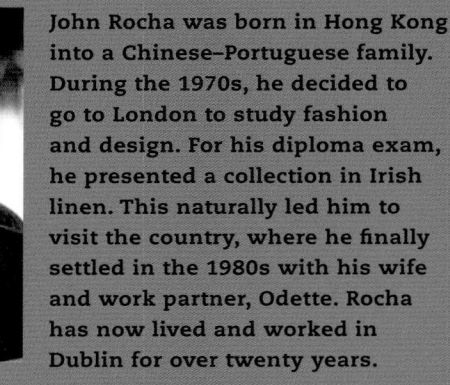

John Rocha was born in Hong Kong into a Chinese–Portuguese family. During the 1970s, he decided to go to London to study fashion and design. For his diploma exam, he presented a collection in Irish linen. This naturally led him to visit the country, where he finally settled in the 1980s with his wife and work partner, Odette. Rocha has now lived and worked in Dublin for over twenty years.

■ For Rocha, the term "designer" encompasses a broad range of activities and modes of expression. A collection for Waterford Crystal in 1997 was his first foray into a world other than fashion—a body of work that was acclaimed by the press and which he is continuing to develop.

■ The opening of the Morrison Hotel in 1999 marked his highly successful involvement in the first of many architectural projects, and he worked on interior design and architectural projects for offices and private houses in Dublin and Liverpool, as well as luxury apartment projects in Birmingham and Budapest.

■ In July 2002, Rocha launched a line of jewelry, which has a modern look inspired by organic shapes. As in all his work, this collection draws inspiration from images in nature, calling to mind cracks in rock and soft, rounded pebbles. The collection is sold at Liberty in London and in many shops worldwide.

■ In October 2002, a book entitled *John Rocha: Texture, Form, Purity, Detail* traced the designer's work in different fields and described the philosophy of style in his fashion creations, jewelry, and interior design work.

■ Rocha won the prestigious British Designer of the Year prize in 1994, and in 2002 received the title of Commander of the British Empire, awarded by the queen in recognition of his contribution to the fashion industry over a long period.

■ Over a career spanning more than two decades, John Rocha has developed a distinctive style not devoid of a certain romantic quality. His exemplary work on the cut of clothes and his fascination with both traditional arts and new materials render his creations unique and constantly renewed.

Agatha Ruiz de la Prada began her professional career in 1981, with a show of her first collection in Madrid. A stylist prodigy of the Spanish Movida, her astonishing dresses were sold at first only in her own Madrid shop, but she was already exhibiting her hand-painted garments and her designs in prestigious galleries in Madrid and Barcelona. Media acclaim soon followed.

■ Ruiz de la Prada—an electrifying, colorful character—is highly sensitive to her own time. She explores styles, shapes, materials, and colors with unmatched inventiveness. A jack-of-all-trades, she can create garments, fashion accessories, perfumes, and jewelry just as easily as toys, stationery, books, household linens, furniture, or ornaments.

■ A lover of contemporary art and of the avant-garde, Ruiz de la Prada applies her modern tastes to her fashion designs, certainly, but also organizes or takes part in many artistic events. In 1998, she created an installation, *Boda* (a tiled wedding dress), for IVAM (the Valencian Institute of Modern Art) and at the same time organized a retrospective exhibition of her own work for Sala Parpalló in Valencia, which moved the next year to the Bilbao Art Center.

"Homage to Chillida," a collection of dresses on themes dear to the great Basque sculptor, was held at the Museo Nacional Centro de Arte Reina Sofía in Madrid in 1997, and at the Würth Museum in Germany in 1999.

■ Ruiz de la Prada has constantly collaborated on many events in both art and advertising, including theater costumes and posters for *La revolución transparente* (*The Transparent Revolution*, 1989) and *La Dama Boba* by Lope de Vega (1997), and album covers, book covers, illustrations for collections of poems and posters, and architectural projects for the interiors of nurseries, maternity hospitals, and shopping centers.

■ In December 1998, a few months before she opened her shop in Paris's sixth arrondissement, Agatha Ruiz de la Prada made her entry to the capital, backed by Christian Tortu, with the presentation at the Carrousel du Louvre of a parade of ephemeral garments, "dressed" at the last moment by the Parisian master florist.

She held women's fashion shows from 2000 to 2002 in the shop, fitted out for this purpose, and in the following years, as part of the French ready-to-wear fashion federation, held shows at the Carrousel du Louvre.

In September 2004, Agatha decided to hold a fashion show in Milan, in the shop she had opened there in October 2003.

■ Established in Madrid since 1993, twice a year Agatha Ruiz de la Prada receives in her Paris shop-studio Spanish artists who fascinate her and with whom she collaborates on projects code-named "AGATHA +"; these have included, so far, AGATHA + Pep Guerrero, + Barbara Juan, + Laboratorio, + Ciuco Gutierrez, + Carmen Molinero, + Michel Bresson, + Mabel Sanz, and + Angel Molina.

Elie Saab was born in Beirut, Lebanon, on July 4, 1964. Interested in couture from his earliest childhood, he was only nine years old when he began cutting out patterns and making sketches for dresses, which he then made for his sisters. After starting studies in this sphere, he quickly got bored, since he had already mastered the art of tailoring. In 1982, at the age of eighteen, he set up his fashion studio in Beirut. A few months later, he presented his first collection to an audience of young women, who were charmed by the talent of this self-taught artist and designer of ultra-feminine dresses.

■ In 1997, Saab entered the Camera Nazionale della Moda (the National Chamber for Italian Fashion) and presented his designs in Rome for three years before being invited, in 2000, by the Chambre Syndicale de la Haute Couture to present his wares in the French capital.

In 1998, he launched his ready-to-wear collection during the Milan fashion week. From then on, orders flooded in and each season saw the opening of new outlets: Paris, London, Madrid, Moscow, Los Angeles, Hong Kong, and others.

The Elie Saab style is a unique mixture of western and eastern cultures. Noble materials—taffeta, organza, sable, and satin—are blended with softer, lighter ones, such as muslin, to give an airy effect, or fine materials, such as lace. Delicate embroidery consisting of spangles, semiprecious stones, and the flash of Swarovski pearls highlighted a collection of refined femininity.

■ From 1999 onward, Saab dressed great international stars of all artistic spheres (from cinema and theater to music and television), including Halle Berry, who wore one of his dresses when receiving the 2002 Oscar for best actress. That year, Saab moved to Paris, in the heart of the golden triangle, opening a fashion salon and showroom.

■ In March 2003, Elie Saab redesigned the interior of the BMW X series, a project carried out on the initiative of BMW Dubai. Later that year, he teamed up with MAC Cosmetics for two seasons, creating a palette of eye shadows inspired by the colors of his fashion collections. He created another palette specially for the actresses nominated for and presenting at the 2004 Oscars.

In September 2003, Elie Saab became a Knight of the National Order of the Cedar in Lebanon, and in June 2004, during "La France Expose" ("France Exhibits") week, the French ambassador to Lebanon organized a reception in the designer's honor.

Saab's wedding dresses have contributed to his international fame. For him, wedding gowns evoke the dreams of young girls, and he wants to help realize those dreams. So when the Pronovias group, which specializes in ready-to-wear wedding gowns, asked him to design its collection in July 2003, he was happy to offer exceptional gowns to a less wealthy clientele.

■ In 2005, Saab inaugurated his new fashion house in the heart of Beirut's rebuilt city center. It contained his workshops, design studio, ready-to-wear and accessories shop, and couture and wedding gown salons.

In October 2005, he presented his ready-to-wear collection at Paris fashion week for the first time. Then, in 2006, he announced that he was moving to new premises, an area of more than 10,750 square feet (1,000 square meters) in the heart of Paris, where the entire range of his brand would be displayed, including ready-to-wear lines and accessories as well as couture collections. The same year, the designer supported a reality television show, *Mission Fashion*, which nominated apprentice models and designers of the year in the Middle East and Maghreb. A lover of architecture and contemporary design, Saab enjoys designing furniture, which can be seen in each of his houses.

■ Saab is also a philanthropist, and takes part in a number of charity events in France: Paris Tout P'tits (a charity for impoverished children), Les Sapins des Créateurs (an exhibition of Christmas trees decorated by fashion designers), La Grande Braderie de la Mode (a steeply discounted sale to benefit AIDS research), UNICEF's Frimousses des Créateurs (a auction of dolls to raise money for vaccinations), charity dinners for Sidaction (a French AIDS awareness organization), evenings for the Red Cross, and the Bal de la Rose in Monte Carlo, Monaco. He is also involved with the Mosaic Foundation in Washington, the battle against cancer in London, and the fight against children's cancer in Beirut.

Junko Shimada

During the 1960s, after finishing her studies at the Sujino Gajen Dressmaker Institute in Tokyo, Junko Shimada visited Paris. She fell under the spell of the capital, and quickly decided to settle there, becoming one of the pioneers of the Japanese design in France. After working as part of the Mafia team, she joined the Cacharel fashion house in 1975 and was put in charge of children's and later men's ready-to-wear clothes.

- A few years later, in 1981, she created her own label—Junko Shimada Design Studio—and presented her first collection in Paris and Tokyo. It was inspired by the striped prints of men's shirts, and created a masculine-feminine effect.
  Junko Shimada was soon described in the press as "the most Parisian of Japanese women."
  Since then, her collections have been shown each season in Paris.
- 1984 marked the opening of her first Parisian shop, in Rue Étienne-Marcel.
- In 1988, she set up Junko Shimada International in Tokyo, which enabled her to develop different licenses.
  In 1999, she decided to launch a men's line in Japan, and in 2001 a new shop opened in Rue Saint-Florentin, Paris.
- Over the years, Junko Shimada opened some twenty shops in Japan. She also had a number of lines under license: 49 Avenue Junko Shimada, an urban line, Black by Junko Shimada, a dressy line, and Mocassin Junko Shimada, a relaxed, sporty line.
  At the same time, other collections under license came out: handbags, jewelry, scarves, and also household items, such as bath towels and bathrobes.
- She celebrated her fiftieth collection in March 2006.
- In her designs, Shimada combines rigorous work on feminine shapes with a boundless creative spirit toward colors and prints. Her collections show a taste for animal hides and leather, which are presented differently each season. She does not hesitate, in certain designs, to use strong, luminous colors such as candy pink, royal blue, and bright yellow on very elegant dresses, but she combines these with supple, comfortable shapes to produce a successful union between exuberant creativity and a very French, ultrafeminine elegance.
  Junko Shimada creates refined ready-to-wear garments that constantly approach haute couture, with its luxurious materials and her original shapes, constantly reinvented.

Giambattista Valli

Giambattista Valli was born in Rome, Italy, in 1966. It was in this city where he spent his childhood that he came to know the beauty of art, and it is to Rome that he turns in moments of doubt.

- In 1974, while still a child, he was astonished by Claudia Cardinale's smile in Visconti's film The Leopard, and Rita Hayworth's smile in Blood and Sand: These were to be his first inspirations.
- It was at school in 1980 that he discovered the drawings of Jean Cocteau. He was thrilled by René Gruau's drawings for Dior and by the colors of Yves Saint Laurent, whom he imitated and copied.
  After spending a year at the European Design Institute, he joined the illustration department of the prestigious Central St. Martins School in London in 1987.
  In 1988, during his first work experience at Roberto Capucci, he attempted to combine his passion for color with the seriousness of the collections.
  He joined Fendi as a stylist on the Fendissime line in 1990. During the 1990s, he worked for Jackie 60 in New York. He became a women's ready-to-wear stylist for the Krizia label in 1995.
- From 1997 to 2004, Giambattista Valli was artistic fashion and ready-to-wear director at the Emanuel Ungaro fashion house. There, he rediscovered the flair that he had developed at Capucci.
  In 2001, he took over as artistic director of the Ungaro Fever line, and he was also responsible for accessories and licensing.
- In 2004, he created the Giambattista Valli label.
  In 2005, he launched the first collection under his own name, and soon he met with considerable commercial success. His first fashion show in Paris was widely acclaimed by the press.
- His idols include the artist Francis Bacon, for whom he has a passion and whose works he finds very moving. He likes the work of Andy Warhol and the photographer Nan Goldin, and the autobiography of Misia Sert. The works of Marcel Proust and Jean-Paul Sartre have helped him understand Parisians, their emotions, their moods, and society.
  He likes Elsa Schiaparelli and Walter Albini for their unconventional side, and Emanuel Ungaro for his generosity both in his designs and in life, as well as for his friendship and for having had confidence in him.
- He loves all the films of Federico Fellini, whose screenplays and costume designs he enjoys.
  His female icons are Jeanne Moreau, Gena Rowlands, Louise Bourgeois, and Jane Birkin, as well as Bianca Jagger and Elsa Peretti.

Diane Von Furstenberg

Diane Von Furstenberg was born in Brussels, Belgium, on December 31, 1945, to a Greek mother and a Russian father. While studying economics at the university of Geneva she met the Austrian-Italian prince Egon Von Furstenberg. They married, and in 1969 moved to New York, where their two children were born.

■ Von Furstenberg began her career in the world of fashion in 1972, with simple dresses made of jersey. Four years later, she had already sold several million of her wrap dresses. It became the symbol for a whole generation of liberated women. Such was its influence that the Metropolitan Museum of Art in New York exhibited it, and it made the cover of the prestigious magazine *Newsweek*. In 1975, Von Furstenberg created her first perfume, Tatiana, named after her daughter.

■ Von Furstenberg moved to Paris in 1985, and for some years abandoned her work to set up a French publishing house, Salvy. She published three books on the art of living: *Beds, The Bath,* and *The Table*.

In 1998, she published her memoirs, entitled *Diane: A Signature Life*.

Her enthusiastic admirers, who were trying to unearth her famous dresses in "vintage " shops, urged her to return to the forefront of the New York scene. In 1997, Von Furstenberg yielded to their entreaties and, in keeping with her motto, "if you want to feel like a woman, wear a dress," created a collection of dresses based on the philosophy of her first hits: the wrap dress. Over the years, she developed a complete collection comprising sportswear, cosmetics, jewelry, luggage, swimwear, and other accessories.

Through her marriage to the American Barry Diller she became a naturalized American. Such was Von Furstenberg's influence that in June 2005 she received the Lifetime Achievement Award from the Council of Fashion Designers of America (CFDA)—of which she was elected president the following year—for the central role she had played throughout her career and for the consistency of her work.

■ While continuing her work, Von Furstenberg is now also a member of a number of associations and plays a prominent role in the Diller–Von Furstenberg Family Foundation, which is devoted to preserving the historic heritage of the city of New York. She appeared in some episodes of the *Project Runway* series for the American Bravo network. Moreover, she designed, in partnership with T-Mobile, a limited series of Sidekick cell phones.

■ Diane Von Furstenberg's label is sold in prestigious shops in more than forty countries and in capitals of fashion such as Paris, Los Angeles, New York, Miami, and London. Her most recently opened shop is in Saint-Tropez.

Today, Von Furstenberg divides her time between New York, Paris, and her house in Connecticut.

A woman of taste, elegant and sophisticated, she creates her feminine collections—where dresses are always the stars—in her own image.

Acknowledgments

Acknowledgments by Marie Bariller:

I would like to begin by thanking all of the fashion designers featured in this book for the trust they had in me, the time they took to help me, and the dreams and inspiration that they diffuse with passion throughout their seductive and captivating worlds. I especially want to thank Mr. Dolce and Mr. Gabbana, who have supported me from the beginning of this project and who so spontaneously offered to contribute their thoughts in the foreword for this book.

I would like to thank Alex Beauchesne and Bärbel Miebach for their photographs in the Catherine Malandrino chapter of this book.

I would like to thank all of the press agents for their help during the creation of this book:
Pascal Colet, Céline Danhier, Asha Mines, Colette Lacoste, Maud Michel, Marie-Ann Capdeville, Ellen Gross, Emanuela Setti, Patti Cohen and Jenny Lee, Josiane Cristofoli and Sonoko Hiramatsu, Lara Pearce and Emma Kavanagh, Zeina Raphael, Varun Rehani, Raymond Cole, Véronique Duquesne, Agatha Szczepaniak, Jessica Nagel, and Marcy Engelman.
I especially want to thank Alberto Cavalli for his kindness.
Thank you to Anh Doung.
Thank you to Thierry Gasse and Lourdes Mecha for their hospitality.

A thousand times thank you to Guillaume de Laubier, who was able to magnificently capture the detail of each interior. Thank you to the whole team at Aubanel and particularly to Anne Serroy and Laura Stioui, who allowed me to make this book.

I would like to thank my family for their unwavering support and notably, Michèle Bariller for her shrewd advice and contribution. I would like to affectionately thank my dear children, Robin and Axel, for the energy that they give me.

Thank you to my friends: Serge Normant for his always warm and caring help, Jean-Jacques Feldman and Danièle Unglik for their wise recommendations, Caroline Varon for her support and patience.

I would like to thank Philippe Azoulay for his confidence in my project and for his encouragement.

Acknowledgments by Guillaume de Laubier:

I would like to thank each designer whose home appears in this book. They all generously agreed to open up their homes to the benevolent intrusion of my camera. We shared the adventure: Determining the composition of a photo, when moved by another perspective that is new, ephemeral, and intense, is never easy and never neutral, but always fruitful.

I would also like to thank, with a special mention to Paul Henri Bizon, those who encouraged me during this long project, not hesitating to share their contacts with me.

Finally, none of this could have been done without the constancy and flexibility of the teams at the Central Color Laboratory, or without the assiduous support of Anne Serroy, Laura Stioui, and Editions Aubanel.

Photography Credits

Interviews:

All of the photographs are by Guillaume de Laubier, except
for the photographs in the chapter on Catherine Malandrino (pages 124–129).

Page 126: © Alex Beauchesne

Page 127 (top left): © Alex Beauchesne

Pages 125, 127 (top right and bottom), 128, and 129: © Bärbel Miebach

Biographies:

Editor, English-language edition: Aiah R. Wieder
Designer and jacket design, English-language edition: Shawn Dahl
Production Manager, English-language edition: Tina Cameron

Translated from the French by Simon Jones

Library of Congress Cataloging-in-Publication Data
Bariller, Marie.
  [Espaces Privés. English]
  Dressing the home: the private spaces of top fashion designers /
by Marie Bariller ; photographs by Guillaume de Laubier ;
foreword by Dolce & Gabbana.
    p. cm.
  ISBN 978-0-8109-9514-7 (hardcover)
  1. Fashion designers—Homes and haunts. 2. Interior decoration.
I. Laubier, Guillaume de. II. Dolce & Gabbana. III. Title.
NK2115.3.F37B37 2008
747—dc22
                            2007029406

Design by Séverine Morizet

Copyright © 2008 Aubanel, an imprint of La Martinière Groupe, Paris
English translation copyright © 2008 Abrams, New York

First published in 2007 under the title Espaces Privés by Aubanel, Paris
Published in North America in 2008 by Abrams, an imprint of Harry N. Abrams, Inc.

Printed and bound in France
10 9 8 7 6 5 4 3 2 1

HNA ▋▋▋▋▋▋
harry n. abrams, inc.
a subsidiary of La Martinière Groupe
115 West 18th Street
New York, NY 10011
www.hnabooks.com